Editor

Erica N. Russikoff, M.A.

Editor in Chief

Ina Massler Levin, M.A.

Creative Director

Karen J. Goldfluss, M.S. Ed.

Cover Artist

Brenda DiAntonis

Imaging

James Edward Grace

Craig Gunnell

Publisher

Mary D. Smith, M.S. Ed.

TCR 2557

STRATE
to use with your
English Language
Learners

Contains TESOL Goals and Standards

- Includes ELL strategies for teachers and students
- Tailored to help ELLs as well as native English speakers
- Provides sample activities and lessons across the content areas

Teacher Created Resources

Author

Tracie I. Heskett, M. Ed.

Teacher Created Resources

6421 Industry Way
Westminster, CA 92683
www.teachercreated.com

ISBN: 978-1-4206-2557-8

© 2012 Teacher Created Resources
Made in U.S.A.

Table of Contents

Table of Contents *(cont.)*

Introduction

Teachers across the country are experiencing increasing numbers of English language learners (ELLs) in their regular education classrooms. As ELL student populations grow, teachers need strategies to reach these students. Many lessons in existing curricula are designed for native speakers of English and are not tailored to support second language acquisition. The lessons and strategies in this book accommodate the needs of ELLs.

Strategies to Use With Your English Language Learners offers teachers ways to teach specific concepts and skills to ELLs and at-risk students in regular education classrooms. This book includes charts with ELL strategies, teaching methods, suggested activities, and sample lessons.

The following are a few of the most frequently asked questions regarding ELL instruction. The answers provided are general; for more specific answers, review the strategies in this book.

How do specific strategies help ELLs?

Literacy strategies support ELLs as they build English proficiency. Supporting students' first language skills helps students develop literacy in English. Effective teaching strategies engage students and increase their motivation to learn.

What should I do if some students already know the lesson content?

Assess students and use that information to design lesson plans and objectives. Determine what students already know and what they need to know. Include ways to differentiate teaching and activities in the lesson if some students already know part of the lesson content. Encourage students to use what they already know to extend ideas and ask questions about the lesson topic.

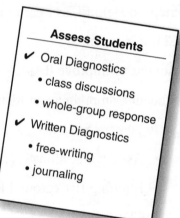

Assess Students

✔ Oral Diagnostics
  • class discussions
  • whole-group response
✔ Written Diagnostics
  • free-writing
  • journaling

How do I reteach if students don't grasp the concept the first time?

Ask questions and check student work throughout the lesson. Provide concrete examples and ask students to give their own examples. Be aware of ways that students' native languages may influence their learning of English. This will allow you to target areas in which students need direct instruction. Try to identify other aspects of the lesson that might cause difficulty for ELLs, and give explanations as needed.

How can I use interactive whiteboard technology to help my ELLs?

Interactive whiteboard technology can be an invaluable resource when working with ELLs. ELL instruction can be visually oriented; pictures, graphics, and other visual information help to increase student comprehension. Use interactive whiteboard technology to enhance the following:

✦ add variety to visual aids and graphic organizers.

✦ provide sentence frames for different language levels.

✦ display charts and tables.

✦ help students make connections between written and oral text.

✦ engage students in cloze activities.

How to Use This Book

The first section, *Developing a Multicultural Classroom*, provides tips and resources to develop a multicultural environment in the classroom. It contains information about working with parents, including a sample parent letter. This section also offers specific steps for integrating English language learners, including how to build cultural awareness, increase verbal interaction, and motivate students.

The second section, *English Language Learner Instruction*, contains information on collaborating with ESL staff, recognizing learning styles, and differentiating lessons. It also addresses specific strategies teachers can use with their ELLs. A few of the strategies you'll find in this section are Environmental Print, Reciprocal Teaching, and TPR. Each strategy page includes an explanation, examples, tips for teaching, and at least one sample activity.

The third section, *Student Literacy Connections*, consists of student and teacher tips to increase literacy, as well as student strategies. Teach your students these strategies so they can use them independently to increase their reading comprehension. A few of the strategies you'll find in this section are Clarifying, Making Inferences, and Using Context Clues. Each strategy page includes an explanation, tips for teaching, and ways to use the strategy across the content areas (reading, writing, social studies, and science).

The final section, *Across the Curriculum*, contains vocabulary tips and activities, acknowledging that students need academic and content-area vocabulary to succeed in school. This section also includes reading, writing, social studies, and science activities; sample lessons; and information on assessment. The resources, activities, and sample lessons provided will help you to incorporate ELL teaching strategies into lessons across the content areas.

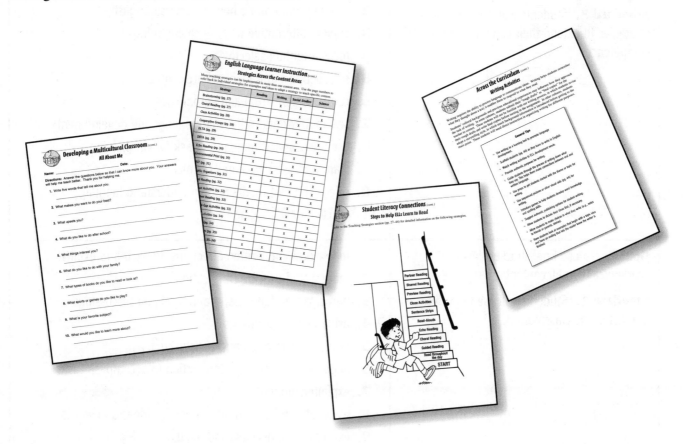

Correlation to TESOL Standards

The following chart lists the Teachers of English to Speakers of Other Languages (TESOL) goals, standards, and descriptors for Pre-K–12 students. (Reprinted with permission of TESOL, from *ESL Standards for Pre-K–12 Students, Online Edition*, 2010; permission conveyed through Copyright Clearance Center, Inc.)

Goals and Standards	Descriptors
Goal 1. To use English to communicate in social settings **Standard 1.** Students will use English to participate in social interactions	1. share and request information 2. express needs, feelings, and ideas 3. use nonverbal communication in social interactions 4. get personal needs met 5. engage in conversations 6. conduct transactions
Goal 1. *(cont.)* **Standard 2.** Students will interact in, through, and with spoken and written English for personal expression and enjoyment	1. describe, read about, or participate in a favorite activity 2. share social and cultural traditions and values 3. express personal needs, feelings, and ideas 4. participate in popular culture
Goal 1. *(cont.)* **Standard 3.** Students will use learning strategies to extend their communicative competence	1. test hypotheses about language 2. listen to and imitate how others use English 3. explore alternative ways of saying things 4. focus attention selectively 5. seek support and feedback from others 6. compare nonverbal and verbal cues 7. self-monitor and self-evaluate language development 8. use the primary language to ask for clarification 9. learn and use language "chunks" 10. select different media to help understand language 11. practice new language
Goal 2. To use English to achieve academically in all content areas **Standard 1.** Students will use English to interact in the classroom	1. follow oral and written directions, implicit and explicit 2. request and provide clarification 3. participate in full class, group, and pair discussions 4. ask and answer questions 5. request information and assistance 6. negotiate and manage interaction to accomplish tasks 7. explain actions 8. elaborate and extend other people's ideas and words 9. express likes, dislikes, and needs

Correlation to TESOL Standards *(cont.)*

Goals and Standards	Descriptors
Goal 2. *(cont.)* **Standard 2.** Students will use English to obtain, process, construct, and provide subject matter information in spoken and written form	1. compare and contrast information 2. persuade, argue, negotiate, evaluate, and justify 3. listen to, speak, read, and write about subject matter information 4. gather information orally and in writing 5. retell information 6. select, connect, and explain information 7. analyze, synthesize, and infer from information 8. respond to the work of peers and others 9. represent information visually and interpret information presented visually 10. hypothesize and make predictions 11. formulate and ask questions 12. understand and produce technical vocabulary and text features according to content area 13. demonstrate knowledge through application in a variety of contexts
Goal 2. *(cont.)* **Standard 3.** Students will use appropriate learning strategies to construct and apply academic knowledge	2. apply basic reading comprehension skills such as skimming, scanning, previewing, and reviewing text 3. use context to construct meaning 4. take notes to record important information and aid one's own learning 6. determine and establish the conditions that help one become an effective learner 7. plan how and when to use cognitive strategies and apply them appropriately to a learning task 8. actively connect new information to information previously learned 9. evaluate one's own success in a completed learning task 10. recognize the need for and seek assistance appropriately from others 11. imitate the behaviors of native English speakers to complete tasks successfully 12. know when to use native language resources to promote understanding

Goals and Standards	Descriptors
Goal 3. To use English in socially and culturally appropriate ways **Standard 1.** Students will use the appropriate language variety, register, and genre according to audience, purpose, and setting	1. use the appropriate degree of formality with different audiences and settings 2. recognize and use standard English and vernacular dialects appropriately 3. use a variety of writing styles appropriate for different audiences, purposes, and settings 4. respond to and use slang appropriately 5. respond to and use idioms appropriately 6. respond to and use humor appropriately 7. determine when it is appropriate to use a language other than English 8. determine appropriate topics for interaction
Goal 3. *(cont.)* **Standard 2.** Students will use nonverbal communication appropriate to audience, purpose, and setting	1. interpret and respond appropriately to nonverbal cues and body language 2. demonstrate knowledge of acceptable nonverbal classroom behaviors 3. use acceptable tone, volume, stress, and intonation in various social settings 4. recognize and adjust behavior in response to nonverbal cues
Goal 3. *(cont.)* **Standard 3.** Students will use appropriate learning strategies to extend their sociolinguistic and sociocultural competence	1. observe and model how others speak and behave in a particular situation or setting 2. experiment with variations of language in social and academic settings 3. seek information about appropriate language use and behavior 4. self-monitor and self-evaluate language use according to setting and audience 5. analyze the social context to determine appropriate language use 6. rehearse variations for language in different social and academic settings 7. decide when use of slang is appropriate

ESL Terms

The following are some of the most common terms used in ESL instruction. These terms are repeated throughout the book. For definitions of specific strategies (e.g., environmental print, scaffolding, context clues), look on pp. 27–44 and 53–71.

Academic language: language used in the school environment, including words, phrases, grammar, and language structure, as well as academic terms and technical language

BICS: Basic Interpersonal Communication Skills (See pg. 12 for an extensive definition.)

Bilingual: speaking two languages fluently

CALP: Cognitive Academic Language Proficiency (See pg. 12 for an extensive definition.)

Chunks/Chunking: information divided into units in order to be more comprehensible

Content area: refers to academic subjects in school (e.g., math, science, English/language arts, reading, and social studies)

Decoding: skills used (such as transfer) to decipher given information into understandable information

Differentiated instruction: modified instruction so that students of different abilities, knowledge, and skills can equally experience materials (e.g., providing multiple assignments within a teaching unit that are tailored for students with differing language levels) (See pg. 25 for more information.)

EFL: English as a Foreign Language

ELL: English Language Learner

ESL: English as a Second Language

Explicit instruction: otherwise known as "direct instruction"; learners are provided with specific information or directions about what is to be learned.

Fluency: ability to read, write, and speak a language easily, naturally, and accurately

Language acquisition: the natural process of learning a language; second language acquisition usually includes formal study

Language proficiency: ability to communicate and understand oral (listening and speaking) and written (reading and writing) academic and nonacademic language (See pg. 10 for the English Language Proficiency levels.)

Multicultural: relating to multiple cultural groups (See pp. 14–21 for information on multicultural classrooms.)

Native language: first language learned and spoken

Native speakers of English (or native English speakers): individuals whose first language is English

Realia: real objects used for tactile demonstrations and for improving students' understanding (e.g., bringing in real fruits and vegetables when teaching fruit and vegetable words)

Transfer (as in language transfer): applying knowledge and skills from a first language to a second language

Wait time: amount of time that elapses between a question or instruction and the next verbal response

Levels of English Language Proficiency

This checklist will help you determine an ELL's proficiency as he or she develops English skills and progresses from one level to the next.

Student Name: _____   **Date:** _____

❑ Level 1–Entering

- ✦ Responds to content-area pictures and graphics
- ✦ Understands and speaks words, phrases, or "chunks" of language (with errors)
- ✦ Understands one-step commands and directions
- ✦ Understands yes-no and WH-questions (pg. 53)
- ✦ Requires visual or graphic support

❑ Level 2–Beginning

- ✦ Responds to general content-area language
- ✦ Understands and speaks phrases and short sentences (with errors)
- ✦ Understands multiple-step commands and directions
- ✦ Understands multiple-step questions and statements
- ✦ Requires some visual or graphic support

❑ Level 3–Developing

- ✦ Responds to general and some specific content-area language
- ✦ Understands, speaks, and writes expanded sentences (with errors)
- ✦ Understands and writes paragraphs (with errors)
- ✦ Requires occasional visual or graphic support

❑ Level 4–Expanding

- ✦ Responds to specific and some technical content-area language
- ✦ Understands, speaks, and writes sentences of varying lengths (with minimal errors)
- ✦ Understands and writes multiple-paragraph assignments (with minimal errors)
- ✦ Requires occasional visual or graphic support

❑ Level 5–Bridging

- ✦ Responds to technical content-area language
- ✦ Understands, speaks, and writes sentences of varying lengths
- ✦ Understands and writes multiple-paragraph stories, essays, or reports
- ✦ Performs close to grade-level expectations in reading, writing, and content-area skills

The Four Language Domains

TESOL's language proficiency standards are divided into four language domains: listening, speaking, reading, and writing. They are listed in the order in which students become proficient. Below each language domain are activities targeted to support language development.

Listening

- ✦ Provide recorded texts for students to practice listening.
- ✦ Have students listen and respond to American TV shows and movies.
- ✦ Provide focused read-aloud experiences.
- ✦ Use puppets.
- ✦ Teach songs and chants for student participation.
- ✦ Read poetry to help students learn how language sounds.
- ✦ Place students in pairs, giving each partner a different list of words or sentences. Have students take turns reading their lists and documenting the words or sentences. Check for accuracy.

Speaking

- ✦ Increase student interaction time.
- ✦ Ask open-ended questions.
- ✦ Have students rehearse a section of text before reading it aloud.
- ✦ Remind students to speak clearly.
- ✦ Provide practice with speaking in different tenses.
- ✦ Encourage students to elaborate on peer responses.
- ✦ Have students participate in dialogues.

Reading

- ✦ Set a purpose for reading.
- ✦ Use a variety of books for a unit of study.
- ✦ Set aside time each day for sustained silent reading (SSR), allowing students to choose their own texts.
- ✦ Teach students how to skim while reading.
- ✦ Have students practice reading songs.
- ✦ Have students practice reading quietly before they read aloud.
- ✦ Have students read subtitles while watching an American TV show.

Writing

- ✦ Model how to use different tenses in writing.
- ✦ Model correct grammar.
- ✦ Help students develop writing skills through practice.
- ✦ Rephrase or expand on what students write.
- ✦ Have students participate in whole-class or small-group writing.
- ✦ Encourage students to practice writing at home.
- ✦ Provide positive feedback.

Types of Language Acquisition: BICS and CALP

ELLs acquire English on two different levels: social and academic. Teachers may hear struggling students speaking naturally with classmates and wonder why they continue to have trouble with schoolwork. It's important to understand that students acquire social language skills (BICS) before academic language proficiency (CALP). What this means is that, although students may be conversationally (BICS) fluent, they have not necessarily mastered academic language skills (CALP). Continue to familiarize your ELLs with classroom concepts in order to increase their academic language proficiency.

BICS–Basic Interpersonal Communication Skills

- ◆ used with friends and family
- ◆ used in face-to-face conversations
- ◆ more informal
- ◆ has short sentences
- ◆ provides contextual clues
- ◆ not cognitively demanding

CALP–Cognitive Academic Language Proficiency

- ◆ used in the classroom and with texts
- ◆ used to express abstract concepts
- ◆ more formal
- ◆ contains complicated grammar, technical vocabulary, and multiple-meaning words
- ◆ lacks context
- ◆ more cognitively demanding
- ◆ may have idioms and figurative language
- ◆ contains words and phrases that describe content-area knowledge and procedures
- ◆ expresses higher-order thinking processes (e.g., inferring, evaluating)

The Importance of CALP in Classroom Instruction

Academic language skills help students to do the following:

- ✦ develop new knowledge.
- ✦ improve literacy.
- ✦ increase test performance.
- ✦ understand abstract concepts.
- ✦ solve problems.
- ✦ make decisions.

- ✦ use written language.
- ✦ use higher-order thinking skills.
- ✦ read textbooks.
- ✦ ask and respond to questions.
- ✦ participate in lessons.
- ✦ work in collaborative groups.

Teachers can help ELLs learn academic language by doing the following:

- ✦ being consistent.
- ✦ reading aloud.
- ✦ providing explicit instruction.
- ✦ recognizing when students need a BICS word to replace a CALP word and modifying the text accordingly.
- ✦ creating a chart of CALP words and related BICS phrases relevant to the classroom and textbooks.
- ✦ introducing and explaining skills daily.
- ✦ targeting instruction to specific skills.
- ✦ clarifying language and vocabulary.
- ✦ explaining the meaning of academic words.
- ✦ rephrasing questions.
- ✦ simplifying texts whenever possible.
- ✦ providing sentence frames that support students' use of academic language.
- ✦ incorporating pair work, allowing students with strong English skills to work with students who need support.
- ✦ following a process; have students listen, paraphrase, and then repeat.
- ✦ showing students how the writing style differs from other written English.
- ✦ showing students how to read academic texts.

CALP words	BICS words
classify	to group
explain	to make clear

Students can learn academic language by doing the following:

- ✦ reading words in context to learn the meaning.
- ✦ looking for visual cues.
- ✦ categorizing words into everyday use and academic use.
- ✦ paying attention to keywords or phrases that are repeated.
- ✦ noticing facial expressions when someone else reads.

Developing a Multicultural Classroom
Home-School Connections

A multicultural classroom is one in which students from a variety of cultural backgrounds feel welcome and safe. Multicultural teachers have an awareness of their students' diverse backgrounds and pass on that cultural awareness to all of their students. As teachers practice empathy and give students opportunities to work in their native languages as well as English, they help students learn a new language. Teachers further build a multicultural environment by encouraging a strong connection between the students' lives at school and at home.

Parents want the best for their children and are concerned about their well-being, particularly at school. Translation resources make it possible for teachers to communicate with family members in their native languages, read notes students bring from home, and allow students to communicate in their native languages as needed to understand new concepts. The following resources can help teachers connect with family members of ELLs:

+ ESL specialists or ESL teachers
+ interpreters
+ bilingual students

+ community members
+ computer programs
+ online resources (pg. 110)

Using these resources, teachers, students, and parents can each help create and maintain a strong, positive connection between home and school.

Specifically, teachers can also do the following:

+ send home a parent note (translated, if necessary) for family discussion to preteach a concept.
+ differentiate between appropriate home and school language.
+ send home pictures of topics of study for home discussion with family members in English or their native languages.
+ teach theme units around ELLs' countries or national food.
+ group students by native language for student conferences and provide interpreters as available.
+ include pictures and other visual aids in parent conferences.
+ encourage parents to hold students accountable for completing homework.

Specifically, students can do the following:

+ ask family members questions about how their cultures relate to topics of study.
+ share family experiences related to topics of current learning.
+ keep reading journals in their native languages.
+ participate in morning share time by sharing experiences through drawings, oral descriptions, or in writing.

Specifically, parents can do the following:

+ share areas of expertise with students through artistic, oral, or written messages.
+ attend morning share time and observe students' interaction.
+ ask students questions in their native languages about what they are learning.
+ assist students with schoolwork by asking questions and discussing assignments in their native languages.
+ attend student conferences (with translation assistance, if necessary).

Developing a Multicultural Classroom *(cont.)*
Sample Parent Letter

Adapt the following letter to fit your teaching situation. Translation assistance may be available for parents who wish to share their experiences with the class. Create a brief explanation of routines, procedures, and expectations specific to your class. As needed, enlist the aid of an ESL specialist or teacher, interpreter, computer software, or online resource to translate parent letters.

Dear Parent or Guardian:

Welcome to our classroom! We hope you and your child will enjoy exploring new learning together.

The following list suggests ways you can help your child do well in school:

- Help your child with homework.

- Ask your child questions, or have him or her read to you.

- Invite your child to ask you questions.

- Ask your child to show you how to do something new that he or she has learned to do.

- Talk with your child about what he or she is learning at school—in any language.

Perhaps you have experience or an area of special knowledge that you can share with our class. You might know how to prepare a special meal or do a particular trade or craft. Perhaps you have another skill or job experience that relates to a current topic of learning. I would like to hear about it. Translation assistance is available, if needed. I look forward to getting to know you better.

Included with this letter is a brief explanation of our classroom procedures. I hope this will help make school easier for your child.

Sincerely,

Developing a Multicultural Classroom (cont.)
8 Steps for Integrating English Language Learners

As teachers receive more and more ELLs into their classrooms, it's important that they learn to integrate them with the rest of their student population. The following eight steps will help you with this process. Instructional goals for ELLs include helping them use English to communicate and learn. As teachers increase their awareness of the cultural diversity their students bring to the classroom, they can get to know and support ELLs as they learn a second language in an academic setting. Comprehensible instruction and opportunities for verbal interaction will motivate students to engage in learning and actively participate in classroom activities.

❶ Create a Supportive Environment

✦ Make students feel comfortable and welcome.

✦ Create a predictable, structured classroom environment.

✦ Hold high expectations and communicate them positively to students.

✦ Help students learn classroom routines.

✦ Tell students your expectations for behavior during group and independent work times.

✦ Write expectations on a chart for display.

❷ Get to Know Your Students

✦ Use formative assessments, such as journals or free-writes.

✦ Use the "All About Me" questionnaire (pg. 20) to learn about your students' interests and backgrounds.

• Help students understand the questions as needed.

• Allow students to draw pictures to represent their answers.

• Have students dictate their responses if they feel more comfortable speaking than writing.

✦ Create a weekly class newsletter. For each edition, focus on a different student.

❸ Build Cultural Awareness

✦ Support and value your students' cultures.

✦ Know which qualities and characteristics a student's culture values.

✦ Understand culturally acceptable ways of intervention in times of community, family tragedy, or student difficulty.

✦ Acknowledge and support diversity.

✦ Know the strengths and benefits of diversity and share them with your students.

✦ Learn a few words and phrases in your students' native languages, if possible.

✦ Build on students' background knowledge (culture, traditions, music, historical figures, family, personal interests).

❸ Build Cultural Awareness *(cont.)*

✦ Connect learning to students' families and cultures.

✦ Use materials that feature students' languages and cultural groups.

✦ Incorporate ways to learn about different cultures into classroom instruction and discussion.

✦ Learn about cultural differences and incorporate them into classroom activities.

✦ Encourage students to share about their cultures with the class.

✦ Allow students to use their native languages for some tasks.

✦ Read multicultural literature in class.

❹ Help Students Learn a New Language

✦ Imagine what it would be like to be an ELL, learning and functioning in a second language.

✦ Enable students to feel secure and willing to take risks with language.

✦ Have students speak in small groups to give them authentic speaking opportunities with real listeners.

✦ Encourage direct responses from students.

✦ Help students to understand that they are adding a new language, not replacing their native languages and cultures.

✦ Increase students' phonemic awareness.

✦ Develop students' knowledge base in their first languages to strengthen their ability to learn a new language.

✦ Teach ELLs the background they need to understand English.

✦ Teach language in context.

✦ Connect words and concepts to students' families and cultures.

✦ Keep a picture dictionary handy for reference.

✦ Label objects in the room.

✦ Offer translation assistance.

❺ Use Comprehensible Instruction

✦ Use simple words and sentences.

✦ Give directions in "chunks."

✦ Preteach vocabulary.

✦ Speak slowly and clearly.

✦ Allow for wait time, or time for students to think, during student responses.

Developing a Multicultural Classroom *(cont.)*

8 Steps for Integrating English Language Learners *(cont.)*

⑤ Use Comprehensible Instruction *(cont.)*

✦ Use repetition, especially in commands and instructions.

✦ Use motions, gestures, and facial expressions to communicate.

✦ Use visual aids (pg. 44).

✦ Build context around a new word or concept.

✦ Question students to make sure they understand concepts and tasks.

✦ Structure lessons to leave enough time for students to practice and demonstrate what they have learned.

✦ Incorporate what students already know into lesson plans.

⑥ Increase Verbal Interaction

✦ Ask open-ended questions.

✦ Provide opportunities for class discussions.

✦ Repeat what students say to show that you understand.

✦ Have students explain how they know which answer is the best choice.

✦ Incorporate partner and group work.

  • Have students interview each other.

  • Number each student with either "1" or "2"; have the first student share with the second student and then switch.

  • Pair an ELL student with a native English speaker.

  • Place students in trios with one ELL student, one student who speaks the ELL's native language and English, and one native English speaker.

✦ Encourage students to communicate ideas and ask questions.

⑦ Provide Opportunities for Active Student Involvement

✦ Engage students in lessons using manipulative materials and realia.

✦ Provide hands-on activities for students so they can learn by doing.

✦ Focus on communication of thoughts and ideas instead of accuracy.

✦ Allow students to practice leadership in classroom activities.

✦ Give students choices of activities and assignments.

✦ Allow students to use methods other than reading and writing to obtain information and express what they have learned.

✦ Give students time to practice speaking.

✦ Include small-group learning activities and learning centers.

❽ Motivate ELLs for Success

◆ Positively reinforce the contributions ELLs make in class.

◆ Provide fun projects and tasks with their own rewards.

◆ Consider classroom contests with prizes, if appropriate.

◆ Plan classroom activities to match student interests and abilities.

◆ Encourage students' desires to impress. Suggest they complete a task with someone they respect as the audience.

◆ Use accountability charts to help students stay on track.

◆ Challenge students and give them reasons to do the following:

- learn the language.

- understand stories.

- establish social relationships and make friends.

- communicate wants, needs, and feelings.

- take part in activities.

- share their cultures with classmates who are native English speakers.

Developing a Multicultural Classroom (cont.)
All About Me

Name: _____ **Date:** _____

Directions: Answer the questions below so that I can know more about you. Your answers will help me teach better. Thank you for helping me.

1. Write five words that tell me about you.

_____

2. What makes you want to do your best?

_____

3. What upsets you?

_____

4. What do you like to do after school?

_____

5. What things interest you?

_____

6. What do you like to do with your family?

_____

7. What types of books do you like to read or look at?

_____

8. What sports or games do you like to play?

_____

9. What is your favorite subject?

_____

10. What would you like to learn more about?

_____

Developing a Multicultural Classroom *(cont.)*
Am I a Multicultural Teacher?

Think about your role in the classroom. Read the questions below and mark a "✔" in the boxes that match your actions. Reflect on the answers to help you better meet your students' needs.

❑ Do I make students feel comfortable and welcome?

❑ Have I created a predictable, structured classroom environment?

❑ Do I hold high expectations and communicate them positively to students?

❑ Do I use formative assessments, such as journals or free-writes?

❑ Have I learned about my students' interests and backgrounds?

❑ Do I support and value my students' cultures?

❑ Do I connect learning to students' families and cultures?

❑ Do I use materials that feature students' languages and cultural groups?

❑ Do I read multicultural literature in class?

❑ Have I imagined what it's like to be an ELL, learning and functioning in a second language?

❑ Do I have students speak in small groups to give them authentic speaking opportunities?

❑ Do I encourage direct responses from students?

❑ Do I preteach vocabulary?

❑ Do I use visual aids?

❑ Do I question students to make sure they understand concepts and tasks?

❑ Do I structure lessons to leave enough time for students to practice and demonstrate what they have learned?

❑ Do I provide opportunities for class discussions?

❑ Do I repeat what students say to show that I understand?

❑ Do I incorporate partner and group work?

❑ Do I engage students in lessons using manipulative materials and realia?

❑ Do I provide hands-on activities for students so they can learn by doing?

❑ Do I focus on communication of thoughts and ideas instead of accuracy?

❑ Do I positively reinforce the contributions ELLs make in class?

❑ Do I use accountability charts to help students stay on track?

❑ Do I challenge students and give them reasons to learn the language?

English Language Learner Instruction
Helping Struggling ELLs

English language learners may quickly fall behind in their comprehension, even though it appears they are completing their work in class. Becoming aware of the needs of ELLs also means knowing when they have difficulty in class. The examples below are representative of students who no longer understand classroom instruction. If you have students that display one or more of the following behaviors, review the Teacher's Responsibilities list below and help your ELLs overcome these obstacles to comprehension.

When students struggle, they may exhibit one or more of the following behaviors:

- ✦ be silent.
- ✦ demonstrate nonverbal behaviors.
- ✦ be inattentive.
- ✦ not feel part of the classroom community.
- ✦ not ask for help.
- ✦ create discipline issues.

- ✦ seek attention.
- ✦ have low reading and writing skills.
- ✦ not understand instruction easily.
- ✦ find it harder to concentrate on the lesson.
- ✦ do poorly on tests.
- ✦ have potential but lack confidence to apply their learning.

Students' Responsibilities	Teacher's Responsibilities
Work hard.	Know your expectations for ELLs and other students.
Find ways to do better.	Provide scaffolding (pg. 40) and partnership for each student.
Ask for help when needed.	Repeat directions or reteach.
Use time well.	Give additional explanation, if needed.
Learn to listen.	Provide wait time, or time for ELLs to respond when prompted, acknowledging that students are processing new information and participating in higher-level thinking.
Participate.	Prompt students to use specific reading strategies.
Help each other.	Observe students during work time and note which students have decoding or comprehension problems.
	Note students' progress in meeting reading and language objectives.
	Intervene quickly when students are off-task, and call on them to participate.
	Work in smaller groups with those students who have difficulty.

English Language Learner Instruction *(cont.)*
Improving ELL Instruction

Provided here are four ways to improve ELL instruction. Collaborating with ESL staff (ESL teachers, counselors, and specialists who have been trained specifically to work with ELLs) will help teachers gain insight and resources to accommodate ELLs in the classroom. Recognizing individual learning styles, planning lessons with ELLs in mind, and differentiating lessons will benefit all students, particularly English language learners. Overall, the tips suggested here will strengthen classroom instruction and ensure that instructional goals and objectives are met.

Collaborate with ESL Staff

- ✦ Use ESL staff as a resource.
- ✦ Participate in linguistic training or professional development opportunities.
- ✦ Collaborate on developing a unit.
- ✦ Co-teach a lesson.
- ✦ Ask for assistance in modifying a teaching strategy before using it in the classroom.
- ✦ Ask for assistance in determining appropriate alternative assessments for your students.
- ✦ Consult them with questions about specific students.
- ✦ Consult them with questions about parent involvement.

Recognize Learning Styles

Students have different learning styles and preferences. Use the teaching strategies described on pp. 27–44 to accommodate a variety of learning styles and meet the needs of your ELLs.

Auditory	Visual
Students learn and remember what they hear. *Appropriate Strategies / Activities:* oral instructions, interviews, oral reading (pg. 36), choral reading (pg. 27), listening tasks, listening jigsaws (pg. 35), information gap activities (pg. 33)	**Students learn and remember what they see.** *Appropriate Strategies / Activities:* written instructions, silent reading, videos, observations, visual aids (pg. 44), graphic organizers (pg. 31), text with pictures
Tactile	**Kinesthetic**
Students learn and remember through touching or feeling. *Appropriate Strategies / Activities:* using manipulatives or realia, drawing, games, modeling (pg. 36)	**Students learn and remember through movement.** *Appropriate Strategies / Activities:* TPR (pg. 44), gestures, movement, role-play, modeling (pg. 36)
Global	**Analytic (Sequential)**
Students are spontaneous and easily bored. They see the big picture but may not understand how they arrive at answers. *Appropriate Strategies / Activities:* cooperative groups (pg. 28), interactive activities (pg. 34), hands-on activities (pg. 32), choral reading (pg. 27), writing stories, games	**Students are organized. They plan their work and learn in logical steps.** *Appropriate Strategies / Activities:* sequencing, individual tasks, clear directions, teacher-directed learning, phonetic activities

Plan Lessons with ELLs in Mind

✦ Use standards as a guide to determine what ELLs need to learn.

✦ Pre-assess students to determine their knowledge and skill levels.

✦ Set instructional goals and learning objectives based on what students still need to know.

✦ Know the purpose for everything you teach or any class activities.

✦ Use strategic lesson planning. Have a beginning, middle, and end.

✦ Determine what students need to do to accomplish learning tasks. Share this information with students.

✦ Preview lesson objectives and activities with students.

- Tell students what they will learn and if they will be reading, writing, listening, or speaking.

- Provide a list of target words for the lesson or unit.

✦ Include one or more strategies to use with your ELLs in each lesson.

✦ Break lessons into "chunks."

✦ Plan how to meet each student's needs.

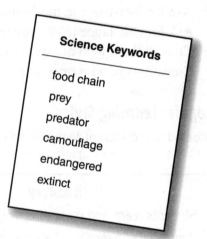

✦ Incorporate what students already know into the lesson plan.

✦ Connect learning in one subject area to learning in another subject area.

✦ Consider all students' backgrounds when planning activities.

✦ Give each activity a name that describes it.

✦ Associate concepts with physical gestures or movements.

✦ Create a visual aid while talking, such as a chart, table, or drawing (pg. 44); use an interactive whiteboard.

✦ Use the same icons throughout a lesson to cue students.

✦ Allow time for students to write notes or give responses.

✦ Have students explain concepts and processes to each other.

✦ Provide a summary and review of the lesson in one or two sentences.

✦ Document student performance to gauge students' needs.

Differentiate Lessons

✦ Differentiate based on skill levels:

- Some students are better speakers.

- Some students are better readers.

- Some students are better writers.

✦ Change the level of instruction, content, or ways students demonstrate performance.

✦ Match lessons and activities to students' learning styles.

✦ Recognize that students may not all be doing the same activity at the same time.

✦ Give students choices of activities when possible.

✦ Provide bilingual activities or resources to help students complete tasks successfully.

✦ Allow students to work at their own pace within guidelines.

✦ Consider behavior management issues.

✦ Address the abilities, needs, interests, and strengths of learners.

✦ Model a concept orally or in writing for the whole class (pg. 36).

✦ Introduce new vocabulary with pictures.

✦ Use technology (e.g., interactive whiteboard) to differentiate instruction.

✦ Use the same reading text for the whole class, adapt activities, and provide direct guided instruction for ELLs.

✦ Adapt required reading activities for two or three levels.

✦ Give students an easy reading task when text is difficult.

✦ Give students a more challenging reading task when the text is easy.

✦ Have students read about the same topic at their own reading levels.

✦ Modify oral tasks based on ELLs' oral fluency.

English Language Learner Instruction *(cont.)*
Tips for Using Teaching Strategies

The following tips will help you integrate strategies when planning lessons:

◆ Use ELL strategies with all students.

◆ Teach students strategies they can use to help themselves learn.

◆ Use sticky tabs to mark pages in order to quickly reference specific strategies.

◆ Write an ELL tip or strategy in your lesson plan book for one or more lessons during the day.

◆ Make cards for the "Extending Vocabulary" strategies (pp. 73–75) or "Strategies Across the Content Areas" (pp. 45–46).

◆ Create cards for any of the other charts in this book as a quick reference.

◆ Consider making cards with various activities for students to choose from based on their learning styles and preferences.

How to incorporate strategy cards into daily teaching:

◆ Keep the cards in a small file box.

◆ Hole-punch cards and place them on a ring for handy reference.

◆ Post one or two cards daily at your desk as a quick visual reminder of strategies to use with ELLs.

◆ Take a few minutes to review one or two cards each morning. In a month, you'll be familiar with several strategies and can draw on them as needed.

English Language Learner Instruction *(cont.)*
Teaching Strategies

Brainstorming

Use this strategy to activate students' prior knowledge. Have students think of as many answers to a question or problem as possible, and then write down everyone's ideas.

Examples: webs, lists (e.g., ways to use an object), clustering, K-W-L charts (pg. 34), mind maps, story maps, diagrams, word association, note-taking, categorizing information (i.e., grouping related items), asking questions (pg. 53), discussing ideas with classmates, drawing pictures to generate ideas

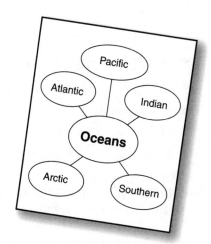

Tips for Teaching the Strategy

- ✦ When compiling students' ideas, make sure everyone can see the diagram.

- ✦ Encourage all students to participate. Model respect for all contributors.

- ✦ Consider a small motivational incentive to encourage ELLs to participate in sharing their ideas aloud.

Sample Activity

Generate a class list of foods that students like to eat. Encourage ELLs to suggest their favorite cultural foods. Consider listing foods for breakfast, lunch, and dinner. Students might be surprised to find out what their classmates prefer to eat for specific meals!

Choral Reading

Use this strategy to increase fluency and reading comprehension skills. Choral reading provides support for struggling readers, encourages them to take risks, and builds their confidence. Have students read in unison as a class or in small groups. Afterwards, discuss the selection and have students re-read the text together.

Ways to Use Choral Reading: for chants, jingles, songs, poetry, readers' theater (pg. 42), nonfiction text (rewritten as scripts), patterned or predictable text, rhyming or rhythmic text

Tips for Teaching the Strategy

- ✦ Use actions and gestures to reinforce the meaning of the text.
- ✦ Use as a differentiated instruction activity by pairing students of different abilities together.
- ✦ Have students take turns leading.

Sample Activity

Have students read a popular song or favorite poem that has a chorus. Have students take turns reading the verses in the role of leader, with the whole class reading the chorus in unison. Rotate students in the role of leaders as time and ability permits.

English Language Learner Instruction (cont.)
Teaching Strategies (cont.)

Cloze Activities

Use this strategy to allow students to actively participate in reading. Prepare a passage with blanks substituted for specific words. Have students substitute words that make sense. Use this strategy in these ways:

- ✦ to teach or review specific aspects of language or grammar.

- ✦ as a pre-reading activity to set a purpose for reading.

- ✦ to engage students in academic reading.

- ✦ to help students learn new words and build vocabulary and comprehension.

- ✦ with or without a word bank.

Examples: fill-in-the-blank passages with word banks, fill-in-the-blank tests, rebus for students

Tips for Teaching the Strategy

- ✦ Cover part of the word or sentence.

- ✦ Provide a word bank.

- ✦ Give the starting letter of the word.

- ✦ Provide written or oral activities.

- ✦ Use with a whole group or have students work independently.

Sample Activity

Work together as a class to have students create a cloze activity or rebus for a partner.

Cooperative Groups

Use this strategy to help students develop critical-thinking skills in a structured learning environment. Cooperative groups focus on student-centered learning and increase student interaction time. Have students work together on a shared task in small groups.

Ways to Use Cooperative Groups: during brainstorming (pg. 27), answering questions, problem solving, projects that demonstrate learning

Tips for Teaching the Strategy

- ✦ Clearly define the task.

- ✦ Assign or rotate individual student roles within the groups.

- ✦ Hold students accountable individually for their own work; have the team turn in a group project, as well.

Sample Activity

Give small groups building blocks and simple pictorial directions. Have students talk with each other to create the model depicted in their set of directions.

English Language Learner Instruction *(cont.)*
Teaching Strategies *(cont.)*

DLTA (Directed Listening-Thinking Activity)

Use this strategy to have students listen to and make predictions throughout a text. This strategy builds on what students already know and shows them how to apply this knowledge to new situations. Teachers should read aloud at the highest level students can understand, bearing in mind that students can comprehend at higher levels than they can read. After reading aloud a passage, invite students to share their predictions. Then, as a class, find evidence in the text that supports their predictions.

Ways to Use DLTA: during the reading of stories or any text students cannot yet read independently

Tip for Teaching the Strategy

Have students make predictions in the form of questions and then notice how those questions were answered in the text.

Sample Activity

Begin reading a picture book. Ask students to make predictions throughout the reading. Then ask for volunteers to share their predictions.

DRTA (Directed Reading-Thinking Activity)

Use this strategy to model how to make and confirm predictions. Here are the steps to DRTA:

1. Choose a text. Preselect stopping points where students can pause while reading.

2. Preview keywords or pictures. Ask questions to guide students' thinking.

3. Have students make predictions about what they will read (pg. 61).

4. Stop at set points so students can check predictions, revise them (as needed), and make new predictions.

5. Ask questions to help students match their predictions to the reading.

6. Discuss what has been read before reading the next section.

Examples: Use objects or pictures to preview a text and make predictions; ask questions about keywords and vocabulary (pg. 53); focus on characters and what they might do.

Tips for Teaching the Strategy
+ Use as a whole-class or small-group activity.
+ Remind students to use what they already know to make predictions.

Sample Activity

Ask students to preview the reading selection with an individual picture walk (pg. 37). Have them write one or two questions they have about the story. Review the students' questions to determine where to stop and discuss the story. Read the selection as a class, pausing as planned. Call on the students who wrote the questions related to that part of the story, and conduct a discussion about the reading thus far.

English Language Learner Instruction (cont.)
Teaching Strategies (cont.)

Echo Reading

Use this strategy to help struggling readers with fluency, pronunciation, intonation, vocabulary, and reading comprehension. The teacher (or other native English speaker) reads the text first, using proper intonation and a good pace. Students follow along silently and then "echo," or imitate, the first reader. Echo reading helps students do the following:

✦ improve sight reading and speaking skills.

✦ build confidence in their pronunciations.

✦ remember important concepts.

Ways to Use Echo Reading: during chants, jingles, songs, poetry, short stories

Tips for Teaching the Strategy

✦ Use gestures to show students which text to read.

✦ Have students who are native English speakers lead the reading; it's helpful for ELLs to hear voices similar to their own.

✦ Adjust the length of text being read to meet the needs of your students. (e.g., For Emerging ELLs, the first reader should read one line of text; for Developing ELLs [and higher levels], the first reader can read several lines of text.)

Sample Activity

Hold a hand to an ear to demonstrate the idea of hearing an echo. Explain that bats use echoes and different tones to locate food sources and other important information. Vary the pitch (higher or lower) while reading to encourage students to practice different intonations when they echo read.

Environmental Print

Use this strategy to connect print materials in home and community settings to those in the classroom. Students read in a known context and add familiar vocabulary. Have students practice the following:

✦ sorting words by categories.

✦ extending vocabulary from a known context to another context.

✦ making connections (pg. 59) between environmental print experiences and authentic literature.

Examples: food containers or wrappers, clothing, signs, other items viewed on a school or neighborhood walk

Tip for Teaching the Strategy

Use environmental print concepts with word walls or picture glossaries.

Sample Activity

Have students recognize and read words based on colors and shapes with the words, for example, the word *fruit* printed on a box of cereal.

English Language Learner Instruction *(cont.)*
Teaching Strategies *(cont.)*

GIST (Generating Interactions Between Schemata and Text)

Use this strategy to help students practice summarizing what they have read. Have students read or listen to a text; circle, highlight, or list keywords (using the 5 Ws and H helps); and write a one- or two-sentence summary using the words.

Ways to Use GIST: in whole-group or small-group activities; groups can trade lists of words and write summary sentences using another group's keywords

Tip for Teaching the Strategy

Use with content-area reading.

Sample Activity

Provide students with simple category charts on which they can write keywords from a passage they read. For example, if students are reading about a farm, the category charts might have headings such as animals, plants (or crops), and actions (what people do). Once all students have completed the reading and identified some keywords, conduct an activity in which students read their words and the teacher compiles a list of commonly identified keywords. Use the class-generated list of words to write one or two summary sentences.

Graphic Organizers

Use this strategy to help students in the following ways:

+ access background knowledge.

+ show relationships between new and existing information.

+ process and organize information while reading.

+ make predictions.

+ summarize learning.

Examples: webs, concept maps, story maps, flow charts, T-charts, sequence chains, timelines, Venn diagrams

Tips for Teaching the Strategy

+ Describe the purpose of the graphic organizer.

+ Make sure ELLs have the language skills required to complete the organizer.

+ Simultaneously model and explain completing a sample organizer.

+ Have students use the graphic organizers independently to complete a task.

+ Have students generate their own graphic organizers to use within their small groups or to share with other students in the class.

Sample Activity

Use a Venn diagram to access background knowledge and compare people groups, for example, the way they live now and what they know about how people lived in the past.

English Language Learner Instruction (cont.)
Teaching Strategies (cont.)

Guided Reading

Use this strategy to help students practice using specific reading strategies. Model reading for students. All students will read the same passage. Have students practice reading the selection with partners and then read it back to a teacher aloud. Support students as they talk about what they have read. Here are the steps to guided reading:

1. Divide students into small groups.

2. Preview a text appropriate to their reading levels. Then read with students using one or more reading strategies.

3. As the students read the text, travel from group to group, providing guidance to individuals based on your observations. (While this interaction takes place, other groups can focus on a literacy activity of your choosing.)

4. After reading, check for understanding by asking questions about the text.

Ways to Use Guided Reading: during stories, short articles, other short passages of informative text; rhyming, rhythmic, or repetitious text

Tips for Teaching the Strategy

✦ Have small groups read fiction or nonfiction texts.

✦ Have students use a pre-reading guide to set a purpose for reading.

✦ Relate guided reading activities to current topics of study in content areas.

✦ Choose to focus on decoding, pronunciation, or grammar skills instead of comprehension skills; use a shared reading activity (pg. 41) to help students focus on meaning.

Sample Activity

Preview a text. Have each student ask a question about the text. Record students' questions on a whiteboard or piece of chart paper. Use guided reading to have students read the text. Invite volunteers to answer one of their classmates' questions after reading.

Hands-on Activities

Use this strategy to provide concrete learning experiences for ELLs. Hands-on activities increase students' participation in class by giving them opportunities to practice speaking and listening.

Examples: multisensory explorations, measurement, graphing, construction, models, experiments, mapping, manipulative materials, craft activities, games

Tip for Teaching the Strategy

Provide clear directions and expectations for students at the start of the activity.

Sample Activity

Place several common objects into a backpack or other opaque container. Invite a volunteer to come up and secretly take an item out of the backpack. The student will hide the object so the class cannot see it. That person will then use descriptive words to tell the class about the object while the students try to guess what it is.

English Language Learner Instruction (cont.)
Teaching Strategies (cont.)

Independent Reading

Use this strategy to allow students to practice reading and comprehending text on their own. Students choose a book to read silently. Provide leveled texts so students can choose appropriate reading material. Help students understand what makes a book "easy" or "hard" so they can make appropriate reading choices.

Examples of Texts to Use With Independent Reading: stories, picture books, nonfiction books, age-appropriate magazines

Tips for Teaching the Strategy

✦ Have students keep reading logs in English or their native languages.

✦ Offer independent reading choices in reading centers with related activities.

✦ Use accelerated reading programs to assess students' reading comprehension.

✦ Model or share how you select a book for independent reading.

Sample Activity

Have students share their independent reading choices with the teacher or adult volunteer during reading conferences or with classmates during partner sharing time.

Information Gap Activities

Use this strategy to strengthen students' listening and speaking skills. One partner (or group) has some information, and the other has the rest of the information. Students must communicate and exchange information to complete their task.

Examples: worksheets, questions, listening jigsaws (pg. 35), reading jigsaws (pg. 39), role-play activities, games

Tips for Teaching the Strategy

✦ Information gap activities can be one-way (with one student having the information to give another student) or two-way (with both students having to share information).

✦ Encourage students to practice asking and answering questions.

Sample Activity

Have students describe a picture or series of shapes to partners who will draw without seeing the original picture.

English Language Learner Instruction *(cont.)*
Teaching Strategies *(cont.)*

Interactive Activities

Use this strategy to increase student interactions and allow students extra practice speaking and reading aloud.

Examples: partner reading (pg. 37), interviews, games, skits (pg. 42), songs, puppets (provide a safe learning experience for students learning BICS skills)

Tip for Teaching the Strategy

Allow students to see the text of the puppet script to aid in listening comprehension.

Sample Activity

Use one or more common objects. Have students take turns placing the object(s) *in* a box, *on* a table, *over* someone's head, etc., to practice using prepositions. Have a group of students work together and arrange themselves to demonstrate prepositions (e.g., *on top of, behind*).

K-W-L Charts

Use this strategy to help students activate what they *know* (K), identify what they *want* (W) to learn, and, after learning the concept, discuss what they have *learned* (L).

Ways to Use K-W-L Charts: in pairs, small groups, or as a whole class; pairs share charts with other pairs; small groups share charts with other small groups; individual students illustrate charts or act out concepts to the class

Tips for Teaching the Strategy

+ Refer to previous classroom concepts to get students thinking about what they already know.

+ Encourage students to make connections.

+ Invite students to explore their curiosity about a topic.

Sample Activity

Have students complete the first column of a K-W-L chart individually. Then ask them to trade papers with partners. Have the partner introduce what the other partner (Zofya) knows about plants, for example, "Zofya knows that plants like sunshine." Have students complete the second column of their charts on their own. Students will trade with a different partner (Moshe) to highlight classmates' thinking. "Moshe wants to learn about plants we can eat." After students have completed the "L" column of the chart, have them tell partners what they learned.

English Language Learner Instruction (cont.)
Teaching Strategies (cont.)

Listening Jigsaws

Use this strategy to divide long audio files into smaller segments for student listening. In this information gap activity, students listen to an audio segment in a small group and then share what they've heard with the whole class. Use podcasts, MP3 technology, or recorded sound clips on computers to provide multiple recordings for students.

Examples: Students hear different excerpts from audio files and share summaries of their segments with the class; students read aloud in small groups and then share their story information with the class.

Tips for Teaching the Strategy

 ✦ This activity requires space for groups to meet before the information exchange.

 ✦ When planning to do a listening jigsaw, consider making your own listening materials. In doing so, you can control the level and content.

 ✦ Consider assigning roles to students within groups, such as reader, clarifier, note-taker, speaker (or reporter). Rotate role cards for each paragraph or section.

 ✦ Have students draw role cards randomly from a container.

Sample Activity

Divide students into small groups. Have students listen to group members read a portion of a selection, for example, from a content-area textbook or reading anthology. Rearrange student groups and have students share the information they learned with classmates in their new groups.

Marking Text

Use this strategy to teach students how to mark text, or make notations, as they read. Marking text allows students to interact with what they read, increasing their comprehension. This strategy helps students to do the following:

 ✦ comprehend what they read.

 ✦ notice grammar and learn patterns of language.

 ✦ identify the main idea and details.

Examples

 ✦ underlining or circling keywords using highlighters, crayons, or colored pencils

 ✦ writing the main idea in the margins

 ✦ marking details that support main ideas

 ✦ writing questions

 ✦ writing a one-sentence summary at the end of each page or section

 ✦ using sticky notes or stars to mark text or pages

 ✦ using colors to identify parts of speech

English Language Learner Instruction *(cont.)*
Teaching Strategies *(cont.)*

Marking Text *(cont.)*

Tips for Teaching the Strategy

- ✦ Give students a purpose for marking text.
- ✦ Use with graphic organizers.
- ✦ Consider making photocopies of text so students can mark freely.
- ✦ Use clear plastic sheets over textbook pages with washable markers.
- ✦ Use scanners and interactive whiteboards to project copies of text.

Sample Activity

Make photocopies of one or two science reading passages and have students write numbers to identify specific aspects of the topic. For example, students could identify characteristics of birds or other categories of things listed in the text.

Modeling

Use this strategy to model, or show by example, how to do something. Modeling provides students with a pattern or guideline to follow and implement in their own learning.

Ways to Use Modeling: through reading strategies, writing techniques, language structures, completing tasks, expectations for classroom behavior, student work

Tips for Teaching the Strategy

- ✦ Set an example and read silently at least one day a week when students read during independent reading time.
- ✦ Talk about your own reading or writing with the class.

Sample Activity

Model a read-aloud (pg. 38) for students.

Oral Reading

Use this strategy to give students repeated opportunities to practice decoding and reading text. Model oral reading for students first. Other students may also model oral reading, especially for ELLs still in the silent phase.

Ways to Use Oral Reading: through target word cards, wordless picture books, environmental print (pg. 30), simple narrative text

Tips for Teaching the Strategy

- ✦ ELLs may use gestures to start.
- ✦ Have students use puppets to read simple text.
- ✦ Use this strategy with group activities.

Sample Activity

Have students practice reading aloud by reading something they have written in their journals during writing time.

English Language Learner Instruction (cont.)
Teaching Strategies (cont.)

Partner Reading

Use this strategy to give students more independent practice reading aloud. Model how to take turns reading, how to help a partner self-correct, and how to ask a partner questions. Have students take turns reading with partners.

Ways to Pair Students: by similar ability, by language proficiency level (e.g., Expanding and Bridging learners can provide support for Entering and Beginning learners.), by native language (bilingual support for clarification)

Tip for Teaching the Strategy

Have students decide how to divide the reading, or assign reading passages to students.

Sample Activity

Have each partner read a different character's dialogue in a story or skit (pg. 42).

Picture Walks

Use this pre-reading strategy to have students look at pictures to predict what a story or text might be about. This strategy helps to generate interest and set a purpose for reading.

Examples: teacher describes each picture, teacher asks students what they see in the pictures, teacher and students take turns describing pictures; small groups discuss pictures and make predictions; pictures are used to introduce new vocabulary

Tips for Teaching the Strategy

✦ Ask students what words they might expect to see in the story based on the pictures they see.

✦ Model enthusiasm for the book.

✦ Call students' attention to challenging words.

Sample Activity

Have students complete a picture walk with partners. Ask volunteers to model the process for the rest of the class. Classmates can provide feedback on the picture walk, such as "I liked the way Amaya described the first picture," or "I think Gregor's prediction will be right."

Read-Alouds

Use this strategy to have students set a purpose for reading and to listen based on that purpose. During read-alouds, the teacher or student(s) reads aloud a passage or story while others listen. Here are the steps to a read-aloud:

1. Read aloud a book that matches the reading levels of your students.

2. Model a specific reading strategy for each lesson.

3. Pose questions for students to think about as they listen.

4. Throughout the read-aloud, have students make predictions, check their predictions, and make new predictions.

Examples of Read-Aloud Materials: word cards, big books, picture books, magazine articles, textbooks, text on charts or interactive whiteboard files

Tips for Teaching the Strategy

✦ Combine a read-aloud with a think-aloud (pp. 42–43) to help students interact with what they hear read aloud.

✦ Provide visual aids to help students learn new vocabulary (pg. 44).

Sample Activity

Introduce the science or social studies topic for the reading. Invite the class to set a purpose for their listening as you read. Perhaps they have a question they would like answered or they are curious about one particular aspect of the topic. Read a short magazine article about the topic, pointing out pictures, captions, headings, and other text features that will guide students in their understanding of the reading. Conduct a class discussion after the reading to review the purpose for reading and determine how the text answered the class question(s).

Reading Guides

Use this strategy to identify the levels of comprehension in students. These teacher-created guides help alert students to text features and other information as they read assigned texts.

Examples: story maps or other graphic organizers (pg. 31), discussion questions to answer, marking text (pp. 35–36)

Tips for Teaching the Strategy

✦ Reading guides may be used as listening guides for a read-aloud (see above) or content-area video.

✦ Give students hand motions to use when they hear specific words or phrases in a story; use movement as a listening guide.

Sample Activity

Provide a list of vocabulary words or specific facts, phrases, or other information for students to find as they read. Have them note the page number on which they read each piece of information.

Reading Jigsaws

Use this strategy to break larger sections of text into smaller sections for student reading. In this information gap activity, students read a passage in small groups and then share what they've read with the whole class.

Examples of Texts to Use With Reading Jigsaws: expository, descriptive, directions for how to do something

Tips for Teaching the Strategy

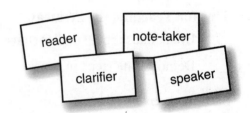

- ✦ Consider assigning roles to students within groups, such as reader, clarifier, note-taker, speaker (or reporter). Rotate role cards for each paragraph or section.

- ✦ Have students draw role cards randomly from a container.

Sample Activity

Divide the class into three groups. Assign each group a different aspect of a topic, for example, food, habitat, and defenses when reading about a particular animal. Have groups read about their subtopics and then describe what they learned to the rest of the class.

Reciprocal Teaching

Use this strategy to help students construct meaning and set a purpose for reading. Using dialogue, the teacher and students will take turns summarizing, generating questions, clarifying, and predicting.

Examples: teacher role reversal, groups with assigned roles, individuals with assigned roles who meet in groups to compare notes, cooperative groups (pg. 28), listening jigsaws (pg. 35), reading jigsaws (see above)

Tips for Teaching the Strategy

- ✦ Use a template or other graphic organizer (pg. 31) to guide students through the process.
- ✦ Guide discussion as needed.
- ✦ Break text into smaller "chunks."
- ✦ Monitor student responses and check for comprehension.

Sample Activity

Use the steps (predict, clarify, ask questions, summarize) in a reading jigsaw activity.

Scaffolding

Use this strategy to help students complete tasks while encouraging them to do as much as they can on their own. Scaffolding acts as a bridge between what the student knows and what the student needs to know to complete a task.

Ways to Use Scaffolding: through visual aids (pg. 44), manipulative materials, realia, examples, lists, tables, graphs, think-alouds (pp. 42–43), paraphrasing (pg. 62), sentence frames (see below)

Tips for Teaching the Strategy

✦ Break a task into smaller steps.

✦ Demonstrate steps in a task.

Sample Activity

Write and say new words to introduce key concepts before giving students dictation. Help students distinguish between sounds by making a two-column list and having students gesture to show the correct number of each word you say. Write on the board the number of words for each sentence in the dictation exercise to guide students.

Sentence Frames

Use this strategy to provide structure for students learning academic language. This strategy gives students phrases that they can complete. Use sentence frames to help students do the following:

✦ complete written work in an activity.

✦ write responses.

✦ compare and contrast.

✦ make connections to prior learning.

✦ make predictions.

Examples: "_____ are alike in these ways"; "_____ are different in these ways"

Tips for Teaching the Strategy

✦ Sentence difficulty should depend on language level. Use simple sentence frames for Entering ELLs, comparative sentence frames for Developing ELLs, and complex-comparative sentence frames for Bridging ELLs.

✦ Write sentence frames on sentence strips or use with an interactive whiteboard.

Sample Activity

Use sentence frames in a get-to-know-you activity to help students feel comfortable writing and speaking English. Use the following frames:

- I am _____ . (Students describe themselves.)
- I have _____ . (Students tell about their families, pets, or favorite items.)
- I like _____ . (Students list a game, sport, food, or other favorite.)

English Language Learner Instruction (cont.)
Teaching Strategies (cont.)

Sentence Patterning

Use this strategy to help students become familiar with sentence patterns. By recognizing basic types of sentence structures in English, students are developing their reading and writing skills.

Ways to Use Sentence Patterning: through chants, cloze activities (pg. 28), sentence charts, rhymes

Tip for Teaching the Strategy

Have students practice using different verb tenses.

Sample Activity

Introduce one or two of the basic sentence structures in the chart, and discuss together as a class. Have students use word tiles or magnets to create different sentences. Suggest a specific topic, if desired.

Basic Sentence Structures	
Subject – Verb	Juan reads.
Subject – Verb – Object	Maki likes rice.
Subject – Verb – Adjective	Dogs are playful.
Subject – Verb – Adverb	School starts today.
Subject – Verb – (Article –) Noun	Mr. Caras is a teacher.

Shared Reading

Use this strategy to encourage students to connect with, anticipate, and make predictions about a text. Shared reading supports readers as they begin to understand details in texts while still focusing on meaning and enjoying what is being read. Shared reading may incorporate another reading strategy, such as echo reading (pg. 30) or choral reading (pg. 27). Here are the steps to this strategy:

1. Preview the text before reading—ask questions and use the text's illustrations to elicit responses and predictions.
2. As you read, check students' predictions against the text of the story.
3. Re-read the book over several days, focusing on a different aspect each time. For example, you may ask students to look for high-frequency, rhyming, or multisyllabic words.
4. Discuss the text after each reading.

Ways to Use Shared Reading: during stories, expository text, poetry, songs

Tips for Teaching the Strategy

✦ Use books with enlarged print and illustrations.

✦ Introduce students to text slightly above their comfort reading levels.

✦ Conduct a read-along activity. Read part of a selection while students follow along, and then have students read.

Sample Activity

Have students take turns reading parts of a selection. Ask each student to say something different about the passage as a whole.

English Language Learner Instruction *(cont.)*
Teaching Strategies *(cont.)*

Simulations

Use this strategy when real-life processes happen too quickly to study, take too long, or are too dangerous, expensive, or inaccessible.

Examples: role-play, puppets, board games, cartoon drawings (on paper), cartoon figures (toys), interactive whiteboard software

Tips for Teaching the Strategy
✦ Explain all the parts of an activity (using visual aids, if needed) before starting.

✦ Give students role cards as needed.

Sample Activity
Have students create a human model and role-play to demonstrate life processes, such as sound waves traveling through the ear.

Skits / Readers' Theater

Use this strategy to give students extra practice before reading aloud in front of the class. Have students practice reading the lines for their roles from a script. Allow students enough time to read their lines multiple times before reading in front of others.

Examples: plays, skits, readers' theater scripts (available from online resources), simple stories rewritten as scripts

Tips for Teaching the Strategy
✦ Have some props available and allow students to use them.

✦ Encourage students to sit in chairs or stand in front of the class to help others hear better.

✦ Rewrite portions of content-area text or have students assist in writing fiction or nonfiction texts.

Sample Activity
Have students write their own scripts based on personal or class experiences.

Think-Alouds

Use this strategy to model thought processes while reading, writing, or demonstrating an activity to students. In doing so, you are showing your problem-solving techniques, which students can reflect on and adopt as their own. Think-alouds also demonstrate to students that they are not alone in having to think their way through tasks. Here are the basic steps to a think-aloud:

1. Choose a book and read it out loud.

2. Stop to make comments while reading.

3. Have students discuss what they observed while you were thinking aloud.

English Language Learner Instruction *(cont.)*
Teaching Strategies *(cont.)*

Think-Alouds *(cont.)*

Alternatively, you can modify the steps using one or several of the following options:

✦ Continue reading, allowing students to stop you at any time and ask what you are thinking.

✦ Reverse the process. Call on a volunteer during whole-class reading, and ask that student what he or she is thinking as he or she reads.

✦ Have students practice with partners or in small groups.

Ways to Use Think-Alouds: when comparing and contrasting (pg. 56), practicing cause and effect, analyzing specific plot events, discussing word patterns

Tips for Teaching the Strategy

✦ Pre-read and place sticky notes to remind yourself of your thoughts as you read.

✦ Plan ahead when to stop and think aloud.

Sample Activity

Begin a read-aloud (pg. 38). After reading the first page, think aloud to ask questions. For example, after reading the first page of *The Ox-Cart Man* (D. Hall, 1979), say, "I wonder what they made or grew all year, and I wonder what was left over. Why would something be left over?" Continue reading the second page and notice how there was wool left over. Think aloud on the third page, by saying, "Wow, they made a lot of things. Will it all fit in the wagon?"

Think-Pair-Share

Use this strategy so ELLs can rehearse what they want to say, negotiate meaning with partners, and expand or correct their understanding. Here are the steps to think-pair-share:

1. Ask a question.

2. Have students think for a moment silently.

3. Ask students to share their ideas with partners.

4. Call on volunteers to share with the class.

Ways to Use Think-Pair-Share: during class discussions; brainstorming (pg. 27); asking questions about narrative stories, textbooks, and nonfiction reading passages

Tips for Teaching the Strategy

✦ Have students turn in their notes to check for gaps in understanding.

✦ Listen carefully to ELLs as they discuss with partners.

Sample Activity

Introduce a map/geography lesson with a question about trips. Ask students where they go with their families (or on vacation). Have them turn and talk with partners to practice saying place names. For fun, have one partner identify the specific place name after the other partner has described the place.

English Language Learner Instruction (cont.)
Teaching Strategies (cont.)

TPR (Total Physical Response)

Use this strategy to incorporate physical movements, as well as the sounds, words, or phrases associated with these movements, into your lessons. Using TPR, students respond physically to commands or statements made by the teacher (e.g., "stand up," "sit down," "jump"). The physical response demonstrates understanding.

Examples: pointing to a picture, object, or word; gestures to express "yes" or "no" to simple questions; a series of body movements to learn a series of sounds or words

Tips for Teaching the Strategy

✦ Use TPR while reading or telling a story.

✦ Keep movements and related words consistent.

✦ Connect specific gestures with phonics or target words.

Sample Activity

Preteach words and vocabulary for a simple activity, for example, coloring and folding a picture. Use gestures and movement to model each step for students.

Visual Aids

Use this strategy to help those who are visual learners "see" what they need to know. Use visual aids to help students clarify meaning and relate new vocabulary and concepts to visual images.

Examples: drawings, diagrams, posters, overhead transparencies, slide shows, videos, illustrated books, magnet pictures/boards, photographs, charts, interactive whiteboard

Tips for Teaching the Strategy

✦ Reproduce copies of lessons for ELLs, if possible.

✦ Use different colors to relate to key points.

Sample Activity

Find pictures that represent current class concepts. Show the pictures and have students name them.

Whole-Group Response

Use this strategy to help students lower their anxiety and gain confidence when providing answers. Because students are not singled out to give responses, they feel more comfortable sharing. For this reason, more students maintain focus and want to respond.

Examples: Have students point to something, raise their hands or fingers, answer in chorus (pg. 27), use body movements or gestures, say chants with motions, etc.

Tip for Teaching the Strategy

Teach the response before applying it to a lesson.

Sample Activity

Have students use body movements as they practice repeating a phonics lesson, with one movement for each letter sound. Put movements together into a brief routine. Scramble the order in which they practice for a combined phonics/exercise activity.

English Language Learner Instruction *(cont.)*
Strategies Across the Content Areas

Many teaching strategies can be implemented in more than one content area. Use the page numbers to refer back to individual strategies for examples and ideas to adapt a strategy to teach specific content.

Strategy	Reading	Writing	Social Studies	Science
Brainstorming (pg. 27)		X	X	X
Choral Reading (pg. 27)	X		X	X
Cloze Activities (pg. 28)	X	X	X	X
Cooperative Groups (pg. 28)	X	X	X	X
DLTA (pg. 29)	X		X	X
DRTA (pg. 29)	X		X	X
Echo Reading (pg. 30)	X		X	X
Environmental Print (pg. 30)	X		X	X
GIST (pg. 31)	X	X	X	X
Graphic Organizers (pg. 31)	X	X	X	X
Guided Reading (pg. 32)	X		X	X
Hands-on Activities (pg. 32)		X	X	X
Independent Reading (pg. 33)	X		X	X
Information Gap Activities (pg. 33)	X		X	X
Interactive Activities (pg. 34)	X		X	X
K-W-L Charts (pg. 34)	X	X	X	X
Listening Jigsaws (pg. 35)	X		X	X
Marking Text (pp. 35–36)	X	X	X	X
Modeling (pg. 36)	X	X	X	X

Strategy	Reading	Writing	Social Studies	Science
Oral Reading (pg. 36)	X		X	X
Partner Reading (pg. 37)	X		X	X
Picture Walks (pg. 37)	X		X	X
Read-Alouds (pg. 38)	X		X	X
Reading Guides (pg. 38)	X	X	X	X
Reading Jigsaws (pg. 39)	X		X	X
Reciprocal Teaching (pg. 39)	X		X	X
Scaffolding (pg. 40)	X	X	X	X
Sentence Frames (pg. 40)	X	X	X	X
Sentence Patterning (pg. 41)	X	X	X	X
Shared Reading (pg. 41)	X		X	X
Simulations (pg. 42)	X		X	X
Skits / Readers' Theater (pg. 42)	X	X	X	X
Think-Alouds (pp. 42–43)	X		X	X
Think-Pair-Share (pg. 43)	X	X	X	X
TPR (pg. 44)	X		X	X
Visual Aids (pg. 44)	X		X	X
Whole-Group Response (pg. 44)	X		X	X

Student Literacy Connections
Understanding Literacy

Literacy refers to the ability to read and write. In a broader sense, it encompasses learning, or making sense out of new information. What we already know determines how we construct meaning from what we read, which helps us to understand the world in which we live.

Literacy is affected by various factors, including family and home environments, music, traditions, technology, etc. As a teacher, it's important to recognize these factors and create a classroom environment that encourages literacy. Consider sharing your individual or family literacy with students by bringing in printed materials from home. Invite students to reciprocate so that you can learn as much as possible about each student's abilities in English.

Increasing literacy is a joint venture. While it's important for teachers to implement teaching strategies, it's just as important for students to adopt some of their own. The following pages include teacher tips for literacy, actions to improve reading comprehension, and strategies for students. Model and teach these strategies to students. Suggest that when they have trouble understanding what they read, they try one of them.

Additionally, the tips below can aid students in monitoring their own comprehension. Consider photocopying and enlarging this list for classroom display.

Student Tips for Literacy

✦ Talk through the thinking and reading process using the following sentence frames:

- I know _____ (title) takes place _____.

- I already know _____ about _____ (topic).

- When I think about the setting, I realize that _____.

- I can use _____ (new information) to _____.

✦ Pause and check for understanding.

✦ Re-read a passage, if necessary.

✦ Read quietly to yourself to focus on, understand, and remember what you read.

✦ Read aloud with a partner to help you understand.

✦ Repeat what you have read to yourself.

✦ Tell someone else what you have read.

✦ Cover up a word that you don't know and try a word that you do know to learn what the new word means.

✦ Find out word meanings. Look up words in a dictionary or ask a teacher, parent, or classmate.

✦ Ask questions as you read.

✦ Guess what you think will happen. Check and change your guesses, if needed.

Teacher Tips for Literacy

✦ Model enjoyment and comprehension of reading.

✦ Use big books to engage students in illustrations and text.

✦ Demonstrate different teaching and student strategies using a variety of texts.

✦ Focus on only one strategy during a reading conference or lesson.

✦ Provide reading experiences for students to help them develop meaning.

✦ Allow students to practice reading a section of text before reading it aloud in front of the class.

✦ Check to see if students express confusion or understanding.

✦ Give students opportunities to express what they think about what they read verbally or in writing.

✦ Teach phonetic skills, such as these:

- sounding out words when reading aloud

- letter-sound relationships

- tips for remembering words and sounds

✦ Preteach the following:

- vocabulary for specific reading skills

- text structures, as needed (e.g., headings, captions)

- skills or concepts

✦ Explain the various purposes of reading:

- to share information

- to learn something new

- to enjoy a story

- to be able to do something

Student Literacy Connections *(cont.)*
Steps to Help ELLs Learn to Read

For detailed information on the following teaching strategies, See pp. 27–44.

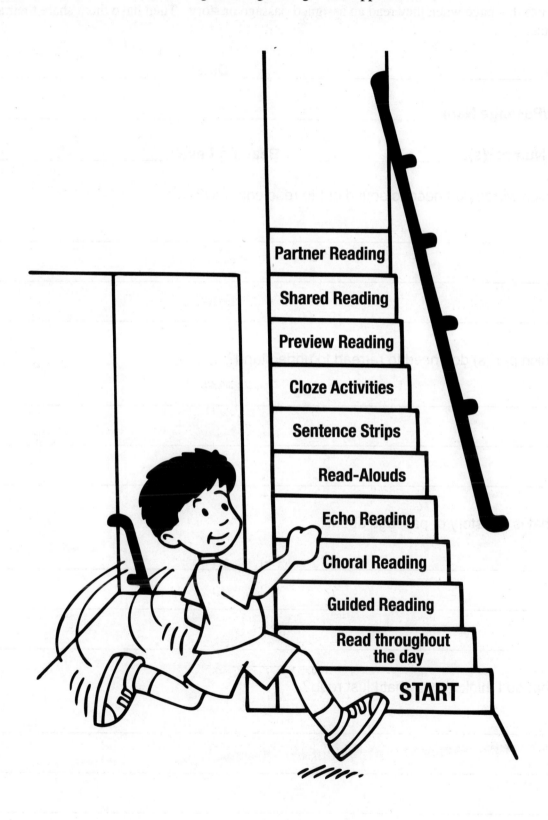

Partner Reading

Shared Reading

Preview Reading

Cloze Activities

Sentence Strips

Read-Alouds

Echo Reading

Choral Reading

Guided Reading

Read throughout the day

START

Student Literacy Connections *(cont.)*
Check Yourself

Reproduce and use this page when listening to students read aloud during a reading conference. Or have students use this page when they read an assigned passage or story. Then have them share their answers with partners.

Name: _____ **Date:** _____

Story/Passage Name: _____

Page Number(s): _____ **Reading Level:** _____

1. Which words do I need to sound out to read correctly?

_____

_____

_____

2. Which part(s) do I need to re-read to understand?

_____

_____

_____

3. What is the story or passage about?

_____

_____

_____

4. What do I think about what I just read?

_____

_____

_____

Student Literacy Connections (cont.)
Actions to Improve Reading Comprehension

The chart below includes actions that teachers and students can perform in order to improve students' overall reading comprehension.

Teacher Actions	Student Actions
Read aloud every day.	Read every day.
Offer a variety of reading choices at or slightly above students' levels.	Read across the content areas.
Implement and model teaching strategies (pp. 27–44).	Whisper-read to help yourself understand what you read.
Teach students how to use student strategies (pp. 53–71).	Re-read familiar texts to improve literacy skills and comprehension.
Focus on and review key concepts from texts.	Give a variety of responses to reading: oral, written, and artistic.
Explain language and content as needed to build on prior knowledge.	Learn and use student strategies (pp. 53–71).
Rewrite passages to break long, complicated sentences into short, simplified sentences.	Discuss texts in your native language if another student speaks the same language.
Use motions, gestures, and visual aids to anchor meaning.	Help classmates with understanding words and phrases when discussing text in a small group.
Ask questions to engage students in direct conversation about reading.	Cover up words you don't know and try replacing them with words you do know to learn what the new words mean.
Use texts with familiar vocabulary.	Ask questions about the text.
Use games and interactive whiteboard activities to develop reading and listening comprehension.	Make guesses while you read. Then check your guesses.
Provide various writing exercises to allow students to interact with text.	Be aware of sentence structures and punctuation in the text.
Provide examples to show students how to interact effectively with expository text.	Use picture cards to practice putting the events of a story in order. Retell the events in your own words to a partner.
Teach students to monitor what they decode and to reflect on what they do and do not understand.	

Student Literacy Connections *(cont.)*
Student Comprehension Identifiers

Use this form as a pre-assessment or post-assessment tool to evaluate students' comprehension. Check the identifiers that apply for each student.

Identifiers

1. Student participates in class discussion but makes no connection to the printed page.
2. Student reads the words but does not understand.
3. Student does not understand oral directions.
4. Student understands oral classroom directions but does not understand written directions.

Date	Student Name	ID 1	ID 2	ID 3	ID 4

Student Literacy Connections (cont.)
Strategies for Students

Asking Questions

Question words help students identify specific information. Students can ask questions about people, places, events, things, quantities, or characteristics. Asking questions helps students interact with text and apply what they learn. Students can ask questions to identify and remember what is important in a selection. They can also use questions to check how well they understand text.

Tips for Teaching the Strategy

✦ Teach the question words: *who, what, where, when, why,* and *how.*

✦ Consider introducing the question words using students' native languages.

✦ Begin by having students ask each other questions in conversation, and then transfer the skill to academic tasks.

✦ Use objects as you ask questions to engage students.

✦ Use sentence frames (pg. 40) to help students complete questions and statements, such as these:

  • When you said _____, did you mean _____?

  • I think you said _____.

  • What I heard you say was _____.

  • From what you said, I understand that _____.

  • I know_____ because it says _____ in the text.

  • I came to the conclusion that _____ because _____.

  • If _____ happened, then _____.

✦ Model asking questions as you read a short selection.

✦ Take this opportunity to begin teaching students how word order changes when asking a question. Give examples.

Activities

Use questions to preview a text. Include questions on the title, chapters, headings, and visual information.

Have students use sticky notes to ask questions as they read with partners or independently. Invite students to share their questions with partners or the whole class to begin a discussion about the reading.

Have students write questions about what they want to find out or what they are curious about in the selection. Have them find the answers as they read.

Have students ask each other questions about stories they read during independent reading time.

Play a game using questions, such as a simplified version of "20 Questions" or "I Spy."

Student Literacy Connections *(cont.)*

Strategies for Students *(cont.)*

Building Background Knowledge

Students build background knowledge when they can relate what they learn in class to something they already know. Teachers help students develop this skill by being aware of how topics connect to their students' lives. It also helps to evaluate or assess students' prior knowledge about a topic before teaching. Provide the background knowledge needed to help students make the transition from what they know to what you want them to learn.

Tips for Teaching the Strategy

Independence Days

U.S.—July 4
India—August 15
Mexico—September 16

+ Relate concepts to students' personal experiences.

+ Help students connect new ideas to what they already know.

+ Consider how the following relate to your students:

  • cultural backgrounds

  • previous educational experiences

  • customs and traditions

+ Encourage students to share their cultural experiences.

+ Have students talk with family members to learn their views on a particular topic.

+ Use resources, such as art, music, and multicultural literature, to involve students in building background knowledge.

+ Encourage peers to activate background knowledge.

+ Use picture books to introduce new concepts.

+ Incorporate environmental print (pg. 30) to build background knowledge.

Activities
Have students participate in a story-telling experience to activate what they already know about a topic.
Read aloud a related text to start thinking about a topic. Have students complete a specific task related to the topic.
Group related ideas into categories to activate students' knowledge about a subject.

Student Literacy Connections (cont.)
Strategies for Students (cont.)

Clarifying

When students have trouble understanding the events in a reading selection, teach them to clarify meaning to increase reading comprehension. Students can re-read, look for visual cues, check the pronunciation of a word they don't know, or read the context to determine the meaning of a new word. It's important that ELLs stop and clarify when they read something they don't understand.

Tips for Teaching the Strategy

✦ Explain key concepts in students' native languages, if possible.

✦ Remind students to use the student actions listed on the "Actions to Improve Reading Comprehension" page (pg. 51)

✦ Have students look for a comma after a word they don't know; the definition of the word may follow.

✦ Show students how to mark text (pp. 35–36).

✦ Think aloud to model how to clarify meaning, using the following steps:

   • ask questions

   • re-read the unknown word

   • say your thought processes out loud

✦ Have students try to connect the text to something else they've read.

✦ Instruct students to look at illustrations to clarify text.

✦ Encourage students to use visualization techniques (pg. 71) to understand what they read.

✦ Simplify written instructions and test directions.

Activities
Ask students to highlight what needs clarification as they read (by underlining or circling unknown words with crayons).
Check that students understand that _____ means _____.
Use "Context Clue Cards" (pg. 70) during a classroom story-telling experience.
Have students interact with classmates using their primary language to help each other clarify meaning when reading.
Use an interactive whiteboard to clarify the content of questions as needed during a lesson.
Have students cover up a new word and substitute a similar word to clarify meaning.

Comparing and Contrasting

We compare when we look for ways in which things are alike. We contrast when we look for ways in which things are different. When students are comparing and contrasting, they are grouping ideas into categories, noticing clues in the text, and clarifying their thinking.

Tips for Teaching the Strategy

✦ Teach the meanings of *compare* and *contrast*, and introduce students to some of the most common signal words.

  • *Compare:* in comparison, at the same time, like, both, similarly

  • *Contrast:* however, but, yet, in contrast, compared with, different from, unlike

✦ Use pictures to introduce this skill and have students practice by orally comparing and contrasting the images.

✦ Help students determine what to compare and contrast before they read.

✦ Instruct students how to use Venn diagrams and T-charts as comparison tools.

✦ Have students mark text (pp. 35–36), using one color to compare and a different color to contrast.

✦ Have students use a Venn diagram or T-chart to compare/contrast their learning and to learn from each other (pg. 31).

✦ Introduce similes as a way to compare things in writing. Explain that authors use similes to help the reader understand something by comparing it to a familiar object. Similes are phrases that use the words *like* or *as* to compare two unlike things. For example, "his shirt was as yellow as the sun."

Activities
Show students examples in which an author compares and contrasts two or more things. Discuss how the things are similar and different.
Have students practice the skill by completing a compare/contrast matrix with two objects. Consider using objects with similar or different colors, shapes, and sizes.
Students can focus on one specific aspect of a story, for example, a character, to compare or contrast it with another story.
As a class, complete a comparison web. Brainstorm things that are only true about A or B. Come back to the similarities, the things that are true for both.
A cloze activity (pg. 28) can help students learn comparative words.
Use color (pencils, crayons, highlighters) to highlight similarities or differences.
Have students discuss with partners or write simple journal entries (one or two sentences) to summarize their comparisons.

Student Literacy Connections *(cont.)*

Strategies for Students *(cont.)*

Finding Main Ideas and Details

Identifying important information in a text will help students determine the main idea, or what the passage is about. Students should be able to state the main idea in one or two sentences. Details that go with the main idea relate specifically to it and give more information about what is happening.

Tips for Teaching the Strategy

✦ Teach the question words used to find details in a text: *who, what, when, where, why,* and *how.*

✦ Use one or more boxes to frame the main idea(s) and bullets to list the details.

✦ Review present and past tenses so students can use the correct tense when reflecting on a reading passage. Help students answer reading questions using the correct tenses.

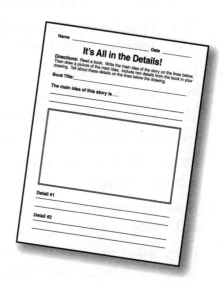

✦ Have students use graphic organizers (pg. 31), such as an outline, to identify the main idea and details.

✦ Ask questions, such as these: "What is this passage about?" "What details help me understand the main idea?" and "What did I learn?"

✦ Teach students how to find keywords.

✦ Study a passage together. Ask students to locate where they found the main idea (e.g., the topic sentence of a paragraph, at the end of the section). Model how to mark text (pp. 35–36) to identify details.

Activities
Have students write simple sentences and add details later.

Have students write simple sentences and add details later.

Have students take notes about the details and then discuss together in small groups to determine the main idea.

Have students state one sentence to describe a picture to someone else, without showing the other person the picture. Then ask them to add details to describe the picture more.

Have students sort concrete examples into categories to determine which "details" go together to support one "main idea."

Student Literacy Connections *(cont.)*
Strategies for Students *(cont.)*

Identifying Facts and Opinions

Facts are true and real; they can be proven true or false. Opinions express personal thoughts, feelings, and favorites. They are not the same for everyone. Texts often contain facts as well as opinions. When students learn the difference between the two, it helps them to understand what they read, sort information, and evaluate what they learn.

Tips for Teaching the Strategy

✦ Teach the meaning of fact and opinion.

   • *Fact:* A fact can be proven true or false. It is true and real.

   • *Opinion:* An opinion expresses what you think about something, how you feel, or what you like or don't like.

✦ Explain that it is possible to look up factual information to find out if it is true or false.

✦ Teach keywords that indicate opinions, such as *think, feel, most, least, best,* and *worst;* opinions have descriptive words.

✦ Show students examples of facts and opinions using a sample passage.

✦ Have students create their own fact/opinion charts based on "What I think" and "What I know."

✦ Discuss the concept that it's OK for one person to think one thing and for someone else to think something different about the same topic as long as everyone recognizes that these are opinions.

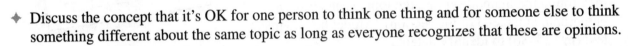

Activities

Read a passage together as a class. Use one color to underline words or phrases that indicate a fact and another color to underline words or phrases that indicate an opinion.

Create a T-chart for a reading selection or topic of current study. List facts on one side and opinions on the other.

Show expressive faces. Have students act out expressions and label them to identify words that express opinions.

Have students participate in a sorting game with sentence strips that have a fact or an opinion listed on each strip.

Have students state a fact and an opinion about an object. Use several different objects.

Student Literacy Connections (cont.)
Strategies for Students (cont.)

Making Connections

Students make connections to what they read when they relate it to their lives, other texts, or the world. They may read a passage that reminds them of something that has happened to them. Or the text may remind them of things they have already read. Or perhaps the text reminds them of a particular place or event. Help students make the following connections: text-to-self, text-to-text, and text-to-world.

Tips for Teaching the Strategy

Text-to-Self

✦ Model a think-aloud (pp. 42–43), demonstrating how to relate text to something you have previously experienced or learned.

✦ Have students draw smiley faces or other graphics to show emotions.

✦ Have students highlight their favorite parts of a passage and tell why they like them.

✦ Encourage students to think about how they feel when they read a passage.

✦ Discuss similarities between the selection and students' prior knowledge.

Text-to-Text

✦ Introduce a story with a picture walk (pg. 37). Ask questions to help students clarify their thinking as they make connections to previous reading.

✦ Discuss with students other texts (including TV shows, movies, games, stories, nonfiction books) that the selection reminds them of.

✦ Model how to ask questions as you read.

✦ Discuss similarities between texts as a class.

Text-to-World

✦ Use graphic organizers (pg. 31) to help students grasp concepts.

✦ Use pictures, visual representations, or actual objects to show connections.

Activities
Help students write journal entries to reflect on what they read.
Help students connect to text by placing themselves in the story. Pose the following question: "How would you feel if you _____?"
Draw a web to link concepts to home, school, family, friends, places visited, or other experiences.
Have students complete sentence frames, such as "This reminds me of _____" and "The text helps me understand _____."
Have students complete Venn diagrams or T-charts to compare texts to other stories, books, songs, or movies.
Use a message board. Have students, teachers, and parents write about (or draw) stories from their lives on a whiteboard or piece of chart paper. Use oral language to describe the written message during a structured circle time.

Making Inferences

Students come to school with a variety of background experiences and language skills. Inference skills help students make accurate predictions about what they read, understand cause-and-effect relationships, and summarize information. Students use the context of what they read combined with what they already know to create meaning. Context clues, such as explanations or details, can help students solve problems, make decisions, or answer questions.

Tips for Teaching the Strategy

✦ Explain that students will look for context clues (pg. 69) to understand more about what a passage means.

✦ Explain that the questions we ask ourselves when we read are natural inference questions. Examples of these are:

   • What caused _____?

   • What do I already know about _____?

   • What do the pictures tell me about what is happening?

   • How has something I have read changed the way I feel about something?

✦ Help students understand the inference process; they make inferences from what the text suggests but doesn't actually say.

✦ Give everyday examples of inference, such as, "If a boy is smiling or laughing, we can infer that he is happy," or "If the text says it is cloudy and a girl has an umbrella, we can infer that it is raining."

✦ Encourage students to notice details in what they read and to use their experiences to help them understand the text.

Activities
Use puppets to talk about a story and share opinions.
Model a think-aloud (pp. 42–43), showing how to make inferences.
Use a cloze activity (pg. 28) to help students understand underlying meanings of a text.
Prepare a reading guide (pg. 38) with inference questions for students to follow during a read-aloud experience.
Read poetry and discuss images and feelings from the reading.
Use a think-pair-share activity (pg. 43) to encourage students to think about what they read and share their thoughts, ideas, and opinions.
Provide word/phrase sentence strips, and have students sort them in a way that makes sense to them. Ask students to explain to partners how and why they sorted their strips the way they did.

Student Literacy Connections (cont.)
Strategies for Students (cont.)

Making Predictions

Making predictions while they read helps students set a purpose for reading. Students use clues, such as the title, cover, pictures, and other text features to think about what will happen in a story. While reading, students should pause at different points in the story and ask themselves if what they have read thus far confirms their predictions. Remind students that their predictions may change as they read. When this is true, they should revise their predictions and then continue reading.

Students can also make predictions before reading a nonfiction text. Encourage them to think about what they already know to predict what new information they might learn as they read. As students read, have them look for words or phrases to confirm their predictions, revising or making new predictions as needed.

Tips for Teaching the Strategy

✦ Model a think-aloud (pp. 42–43), making predictions for fiction or nonfiction text.

✦ Write the steps of the strategy in order, and explain to students how to do the following:
- predict (what you think will happen in a story or what you think you will learn)
- confirm (check to see if your predictions were correct)
- self-correct (make new predictions based on what you read)

✦ Have students be alert to picture clues.

✦ Remind students to use what they already know (background knowledge) to help them make predictions.

✦ Give students a sentence or two from the text in their native languages. Have them work with partners to make predictions. Students will read the remainder of the text in English to check their predictions.

Activities
Create a game using sample paragraphs or situations for students to guess what will happen next.

Have students follow a reading guide (pg. 38) to check their predictions as they read.

Read a passage aloud and have students draw pictures to predict what will happen next.

Use a Directed Reading-Thinking Activity (pg. 29).

Invite students to create an "I Notice" chart when previewing nonfiction text.

Provide sentence frames, such as the following, for students to write simple predictions:

- In this story, I think the main character will _____.

- In this picture, it looks like the character is _____.

- After _____ happens, the next thing that will happen is _____.

Student Literacy Connections (cont.)
Strategies for Students (cont.)

Paraphrasing

One way to help students construct meaning is to paraphrase a text or concept. ELLs benefit from having key phrases or ideas stated in many different ways. Teachers can say or write concepts using different words or restate the definitions of new words.

Tips for Teaching the Strategy

- Model how to paraphrase.

- Tell students that when they paraphrase, they say the same thing but use different words.

- Introduce related vocabulary that has similar meanings.

- Help students identify the main idea of a text and then paraphrase it.

- Teach students to use this skill to check their understanding of what they read.

- Have students restate a statement, question, or direction to verify understanding.

Activities
Have students read a short passage. Ask them to set the original aside and say or write what they have read.
Use paraphrasing to teach new vocabulary.
Use paraphrasing to repeat concepts.
Make a game out of paraphrasing practice.
List question words (*who, what, where, when, why, how*) prior to reading a selection. Have students answer the questions to paraphrase what they read.
Have students use sentence strips to paraphrase a short reading selection, with different students contributing for each strip.
Give each student a word related to a current topic. Have them take turns describing their word to the class without saying the actual word. Classmates will try to guess what the word is.

Student Literacy Connections (cont.)
Strategies for Students (cont.)

Summarizing

A summary restates the main points in a few sentences. It gives the general idea of a reading selection in a shorter form. When students summarize what they read, they use the skill of paraphrasing, or stating something in their own words. Learning to summarize helps students communicate to others what they read and learn.

Tips for Teaching the Strategy

- Help students use graphic organizers to identify main points.

- Model summarizing by rephrasing a text's most important ideas in one or two sentences.

- Review at the end of each chapter or section to practice summarizing as a class.

- Allow students to practice on texts at their levels.

- Have students mark text (pp. 35–36) to identify main ideas and supporting details.

- Have students use visualizing techniques (pg. 71) to help them summarize what they read.

Activities
As a class, create a web in reverse—fill in the details first, then summarize the main idea in the center circle.
Give students a list of words and have them identify a category that would fit all the words.
Give students several sentences about one topic and have students name the topic.
Allow students to orally retell a story and then draw pictures to retell the story. Encourage students to add labels, words, or phrases to their drawings depending on their ability levels.
Have students retell stories aloud in their own words.
Have students orally rehearse a nonfiction summary before writing.
Use a reading jigsaw (pg. 39), and have students summarize their parts of the reading before going on to the next step or task in the process.
Have students number a set of pictures that summarize events in a story.
Have students match words or sentences with pictures from a story or nonfiction passage.

Student Literacy Connections *(cont.)*

Strategies for Students *(cont.)*

Understanding Nonfiction Text Structures

Nonfiction writing, often called expository text, informs or describes. This type of writing appears in many forms, including textbooks, encyclopedias, magazine and newspaper articles, websites, and interviews. Each nonfiction text has a specific organizational structure, as well as text features, such as titles, chapters, headings, graphics, captions, and different types of print. Textbooks and other print materials are classroom tools; teach students how to use these tools just as you would teach them how to use other equipment in the classroom.

Tips for Teaching the Strategy

- ✦ Model a think-aloud (pp. 42–43), showing how "good readers" get information from text.
- ✦ Present text in alternative formats, if necessary.
- ✦ Deconstruct text to show its organization and specific features.
- ✦ Read aloud to preview a section or a chapter of a textbook to review text features.
- ✦ Describe how nonfiction text is structured. Use "Organizational Structures of Nonfiction Text" (pg. 65) as a reference.
- ✦ Use the "Sample Glossary" (pg. 66) to teach related vocabulary.
- ✦ Use the "Sample Textbook Page" (pg. 67) to introduce text features.
- ✦ Prepare a sample reading guide for students to use when they read nonfiction text. Use the "Sample Reading Guide" (pg. 68) as a reference.
- ✦ Help students notice sentence structures in texts to help them understand what they read.

Activities
Provide a graphic organizer (pg. 31) for students to organize information they learn from the text.
Walk through a page of expository text together as a class. Ask the questions listed on "Text Features Questions" (pg. 66). Rewrite the questions as sentence frames or multiple-choice items to meet the needs of your students.
Have students copy a diagram from a textbook page and write their own captions for their drawings.
Enlarge a page of expository text. Place numbers by various textbook features, such as headings, captions, italics, bold print, etc. Provide word cards for each item. Have students work with partners to number their word cards to match the numbers on the displayed example.

Understanding Nonfiction Text Structures *(cont.)*

Organizational Structures of Nonfiction Text	
Cause and Effect	Explains why something happens *Teaching Tip:* Provide a physical demonstration, such as popping a balloon.
Chronological Order	Presents events in the order in which they happened *Teaching Tip:* Describe a typical school day, emphasizing the order of subjects, recess, lunch, etc.
Classification	Describes common attributes of things *Teaching Tip:* Show different fruits and vegetables. (You may want to avoid the tricky ones!) Discuss whether they are fruits or vegetables.
Compare and Contrast	Describes how things are alike and/or different *Teaching Tip:* Use a Venn diagram or matrix to compare and contrast two different pictures of houses. (Perhaps the houses are different but other characteristics, such as a fence or green yard, are the same.)
Descriptive	Describes specific characteristics of a subject *Teaching Tip:* Post a work of art, such as Diego Rivera's *The Flower Carrier* or Leonardo da Vinci's *Mona Lisa*, and describe away!
Graphics	Uses charts, graphs, tables, diagrams, photos, and captions to share information *Teaching Tip:* Share a picture book with the class. Discuss how the pictures help to tell the story.
Persuasive	Tries to get readers to agree with a particular idea or viewpoint *Teaching Tip:* Discuss a TV commercial, including its effects.
Problem and Solution	Asks questions about how to change a difficult situation, and suggests ways to solve the problem *Teaching Tip:* Offer students a sample problem, such as "Bruno's pencil broke." Then provide a solution, such as "Lina gave him one of her pencils."
Process	Describes how something happens *Teaching Tip:* Describe how to cook/make something, such as a peanut butter and jelly sandwich.
Spatial Order	Describes things in physical relation to other things; describes a place *Teaching Tip:* Direct students to an area of the classroom that contains many objects. Describe their placement.

Student Literacy Connections *(cont.)*
Strategies for Students *(cont.)*

Understanding Nonfiction Text Structures: Sample Glossary and Text Features Questions

Photocopy and have students fold this page so the questions are hidden from view. Use the glossary to introduce and explain nonfiction text features and related vocabulary. Then have students unfold the page and review the features using the sample questions.

Glossary

bold print: letters or words that have heavy black lines

bullet: a small dot (or other symbol) used for emphasis at the beginning of a line of text

caption: a short title or description printed below a picture or drawing

chart: a drawing that shows information in the form of a table or graph

diagram: a drawing that explains something

glossary: one or more pages that give the meaning of certain words or phrases used in a book

graph: a diagram that shows the relationship between numbers or amounts

graphics: images such as drawings, maps, or graphs

heading: words written at the top of a page or over a section of writing in a magazine or book

italics: a slanted form of print used to emphasize certain words

map: a detailed plan of an area

picture: an image of something, such as a painting, photograph, or drawing

sidebar: a short article printed alongside a major news story that is a related subject

table: a chart that lists facts and figures, usually in columns

title: the name given to a book or chapter to identify or describe it

---

Text Features Questions

1. Where do you find the heading?

2. Why are titles important?

3. If I want to know what a word means, I can look in the _____.

4. Name two types of graphics.

5. How do captions relate to pictures?

6. Why might an author use bold print or italics?

Understanding Nonfiction Text Structures: Sample Textbook Page

Photocopy and use this sample textbook page (reading level 1.1) to introduce and explain nonfiction text features. Alternatively, use this page as a guide to label a photocopied page from a classroom textbook to provide students with familiar text.

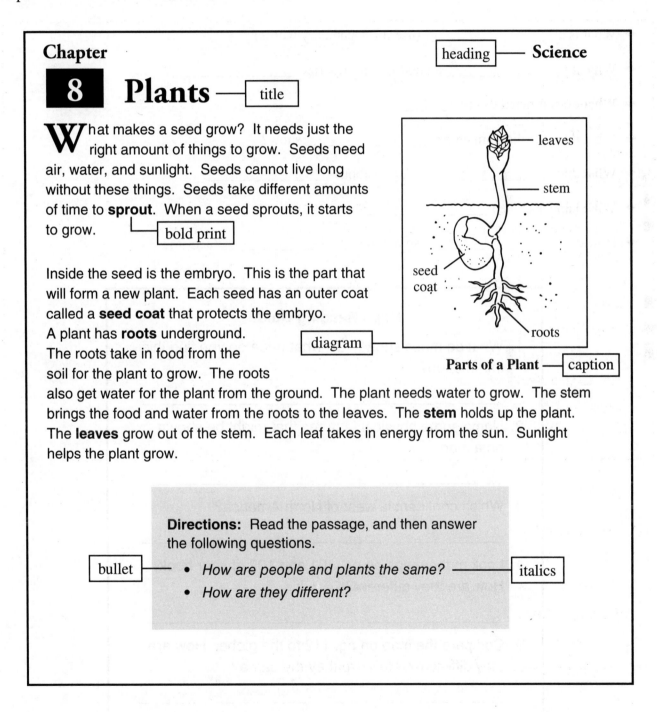

Chapter

8 Plants — title

heading — **Science**

What makes a seed grow? It needs just the right amount of things to grow. Seeds need air, water, and sunlight. Seeds cannot live long without these things. Seeds take different amounts of time to **sprout**. When a seed sprouts, it starts to grow. — bold print

Inside the seed is the embryo. This is the part that will form a new plant. Each seed has an outer coat called a **seed coat** that protects the embryo. A plant has **roots** underground. The roots take in food from the soil for the plant to grow. The roots — diagram

also get water for the plant from the ground. The plant needs water to grow. The stem brings the food and water from the roots to the leaves. The **stem** holds up the plant. The **leaves** grow out of the stem. Each leaf takes in energy from the sun. Sunlight helps the plant grow.

leaves

stem

seed coat

roots

Parts of a Plant — caption

Directions: Read the passage, and then answer the following questions.

bullet — • *How are people and plants the same?* — italics
• *How are they different?*

Student Literacy Connections *(cont.)*

Strategies for Students *(cont.)*

Understanding Nonfiction Text Structures: Sample Reading Guide

Use this page as a reference when creating a reading guide for students. Each reading guide is specific to one textbook passage or reading selection and may have questions or statements that require students to supply one or more words. For more information on reading guides, see pg. 38.

- ✦ What is a _____? (use for vocabulary words)

- ✦ Why is _____ a good way to describe _____?

- ✦ What does it mean to say _____?

- ✦ What does the diagram on pg. _____ show?

- ✦ What does _____ tell you about _____?

- ✦ What happens when _____?

- ✦ How does _____ (something) _____ (action)?

Maps Reading Guide

1. What do maps show? On what page do you find this information?

   _____

2. Name some physical features that might be shown on a map.

   _____

3. Which continent is west of North America?

   _____

4. Look at the maps on pp. 101 and 102 of your book. How are they different?

   _____

5. Compare the map on pg. 112 to the globe. How are they different? How are they the same?

   _____

Student Literacy Connections *(cont.)*
Strategies for Students *(cont.)*

Using Context Clues

Authors often use other words or phrases to help readers define new words. Students can use these clues to help them understand the meaning of what they read. Visual cues, such as pictures, charts, tables, and graphs can also provide clues to the text. Other context clues include punctuation, details, and examples. Context clues help students learn to read critically.

Tips for Teaching the Strategy

✦ Teach only one type of context clue at a time. Use the cards on the next page, if desired.

✦ Provide examples for each type of context clue.

✦ Model with a think-aloud (pp. 42–43) to show how to use context clues.

✦ Show students how to use picture clues to understand what they read.

✦ Show students how to use surrounding text to decode the meanings of new words by substituting words that might make sense in the sentence.

✦ Encourage students to use their background knowledge along with context clues.

✦ Help students identify patterns in a text.

✦ Have students identify examples that explain the concept.

✦ Help students use word association to understand what they read. If they read a selection about dogs, they will expect to find words related to dogs, such as *tail*, *bark*, or *wag*.

Activities
Use one of the brainstorming activities (pg. 27) to discuss as a class what students can do when they encounter words or phrases they don't understand while reading.

Allow students to play with language by changing one or more words in a short passage to a nonsense word. Invite students to guess what the word must mean based on context clues (e.g., parts of speech, illustrations, surrounding words and sentences).

Use cloze activities (pg. 28).

Create cards with icons to use as visual reminders of different types of context clues, which can be used when reading. |

Context Clue Cards

Use the cards below to teach different types of context clues. The cards in the right column are definitions for the cards in the left column. You can copy the page and glue each card pair together, or keep the cards separate to use as a matching activity.

Details and Explanations	An unknown word is defined using reasons or features.
Definition	An unknown word is defined.
Restatement	An unknown word is repeated in a different way (e.g., synonym, antonym).
Examples	An unknown word is defined using details.
Pictures	A drawing, chart, table, or graph gives information about an unknown word.
Punctuation	Commas or other marks can signal an example or detail about an unknown word.
Word Substitution	An unknown word is replaced with a known word to learn the meaning of the unknown word.

Visualizing

Visualization helps students understand story structure. As they create pictures in their minds, students visualize what is happening in a story, which helps their comprehension. They use their senses as they imagine the scenes, allowing them to engage with the text. When students visualize, they also make connections with their prior knowledge.

Tips for Teaching the Strategy

✦ Sketch words while modeling a think-aloud (pp. 42–43).

✦ Point to a picture and ask students simple questions, such as the following, to help them match what they see with what they imagine: "Do you see _____?" and "What does it make you think of?"

✦ Have students close their eyes and form mental pictures as you read. Start with a short selection with vivid descriptions.

✦ Read a passage with concrete objects. Invite students to visualize the shapes, colors, and spatial relationships of the objects. If there is any movement in the passage, have students describe that, as well.

✦ Check student drawings to monitor comprehension.

Activities
Have students listen to a read-aloud (pg. 38). Ask them to draw one or more pictures to show what they heard. Then have students tell partners about their drawings and why they drew the pictures.
Have students listen to a read-aloud and form mental pictures. After they imagine their pictures, have them check or confirm their predictions, if applicable.
Have students focus on visualizing just one specific story element at a time.
Provide a reading guide (pg. 38) to help students create mental pictures as they listen to nonfiction text read aloud.
Divide student papers into sections that correspond to key segments in the book. Read one segment at a time, and have students draw pictures or write keywords related to each segment.
Use graphic organizers (pg. 31) to help students organize and describe mental images.
Use songs to help students practice visualization skills.
Use visualization techniques with readers' theater (pg. 42) or other scripts. Have students draw scenes after they hear about them.

Across the Curriculum
Language Objectives

Language objectives should incorporate the standards students will meet as they learn to use English in academic settings. Include language objectives as part of lessons to help students learn the words and grammatical structures they will need to access and make meaning out of academic content.

✦ Know what you want students to learn.

✦ Incorporate language objectives as part of content-area lesson plans.

✦ Refer to ELL standards to write language objectives.

✦ Be as specific as possible.

✦ Relate objectives to the lesson.

✦ Language objectives include discipline-specific language, academic language, and how language is used in the classroom.

✦ Consider the four language domains when writing language objectives: listening, speaking, reading, and writing.

✦ Help students meet language objectives by checking for understanding, summarizing, and defining terms and concepts as you teach.

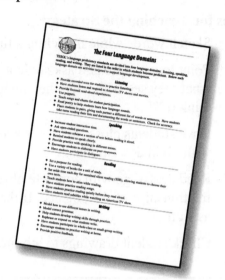

Examples of Language Objectives

✦ Students will write in complete sentences using capital letters and ending punctuation marks.

✦ Students will verbally describe the life cycle of a butterfly.

✦ Students will read their assigned passage and give verbal summaries in groups.

Across the Curriculum (cont.)
Extending Vocabulary

Much of the academic vocabulary students need to learn applies to multiple content areas. Make instruction more comprehensible by using the provided strategies and activities below to help students extend their vocabulary in meaningful ways.

Create an awareness of words.

◆ Create a word-rich environment.

◆ Introduce new words with flash cards.

◆ Design a chart with simple terms to define content-area vocabulary.

◆ Ask students what they notice about a word.

◆ Model a think-aloud (pp. 42–43), showing how to use rhyming strategies.

◆ Provide pictures for concepts with basic vocabulary that corresponds to concepts.

◆ Have students create a symbol or sketch to help them remember what a word means.

◆ Connect vocabulary to prior knowledge.

◆ Give students a purpose for learning new words.

◆ Actively engage students in learning new vocabulary.

◆ Make connections to students' cultures and personal experiences (pg. 59).

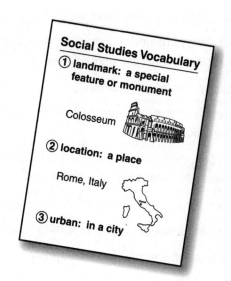

Teach vocabulary in context.

◆ Help students infer word meanings from context.

◆ Help students understand the meaning of a word as it is used in context or in a question.

◆ Encourage students to think about how to use the word.

◆ Apply new vocabulary in a familiar context.

◆ Draw students' attention to any visual clues provided in the context.

◆ Have students complete sentence frames (pg. 40).

◆ Create ways for students to use new words in a variety of contexts.

◆ Use focused questions to assess students' understanding of new words used in context.

Give students direct instruction.

◆ Provide meaningful definitions for new words.

◆ Preteach vocabulary and concepts in small groups, prior to the whole-class lesson. Use materials in ELLs' native languages or at their levels of English proficiency, if possible.

◆ Preteach discipline-specific words, such as *work* (science) and *power* (social studies).

Give students direct instruction. *(cont.)*

✦ Use gestures or hand motions to preteach vocabulary. Have students mimic the gestures.

✦ Use visual aids to explain terms (pg. 44).

✦ Teach language structures and content words on a daily basis.

✦ Model ways to understand new words (pg. 36). Look for punctuation and other context clues, use prior knowledge, use a glossary or dictionary, ask for help, etc.

✦ Explain compound words.

✦ Preteach common command verbs, such as *describe* and *explain*, so students understand what is being asked of them.

✦ Preteach, demonstrate, and explain idioms and special phrases. Compare the literal meaning and the intended meaning, if appropriate.

✦ Check for understanding of vocabulary or content-area words.

✦ Teach students about homophones and homographs.

✦ Teach transition words and sequence words, such as the following:

• after(wards)	• last(ly)
• also	• more(over)
• although	• next
• and	• now
• at first	• or
• at last	• second
• because	• since
• before	• so
• but	• soon
• finally	• then
• first	• third
• for	• though
• however	• until
• if	• while
• in other words	• yet

Incorporate vocabulary instruction throughout the day.

✦ Use simple, everyday language to teach students the meanings of new words.

✦ Draw or illustrate new words.

✦ Label classroom items.

✦ Demonstrate actions or show action items (realia).

✦ Help students learn oral and written versions of words at the same time.

✦ Have students write and pronounce new words correctly as a group.

✦ Have students use new vocabulary in speaking practice in the classroom.

✦ Apply learned vocabulary to new instructional topics.

✦ Expose students to new words in different formats and contexts.

✦ Encourage students to ask questions about words. Then expand on students' questions to define specific terms.

✦ Have classmates explain new terms to each other.

✦ Encourage students to share new, appropriate words they have learned outside of class, at home, and in the community.

✦ Create word webs to expand vocabulary. Warm up with a think-pair-share activity (pg. 43) to get students thinking about the topic.

Activities to Extend Vocabulary

✦ Have students make a list of their favorite words and include pictures or drawings.

✦ Have students classify and sort words by spelling patterns.

✦ Have students write descriptions of vocabulary picture cards.

✦ Allow students to perform skits (pg. 42).

✦ Offer true/false vocabulary questions.

✦ Play a matching game where students have to match words to the appropriate definitions.

✦ Engage students with multiple-choice activities to learn word meanings.

✦ Give students credit for finding vocabulary word(s) used in real-world situations. Have students write down the word, its definition, and where it was heard.

✦ Have students work together to create a word mural. Students will incorporate visual cues and the ways the words might be used, along with definitions.

✦ Use word walls for the following reasons:

• to introduce students to word patterns.

• so students can easily arrange words into categories.

• so students can post words that have meaning for them.

Name _____ Matt _____ Date __8/26__

Real-World Words

Word: legacy

Definition: what is left behind after someone dies

Where It Was Heard: The TV show Clone Wars (episode 10, season 4)— The episode began with the quotation "Our actions define our legacy."

Across the Curriculum (cont.)
Making Sense Out of Textbooks

Most textbooks are written in academic language. Passages have complex sentence structures and specific terms ELL students may not understand. Textbooks also assume that readers have background knowledge in specific areas. Help ELLs navigate textbooks using the following suggestions.

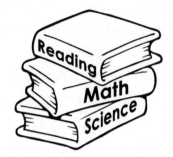

- ✦ Preview text features.

- ✦ Have students make predictions (pg. 61) about the text.

- ✦ Adapt textbook reading.

- ✦ Modify language as needed.

- ✦ Use simple descriptions.

- ✦ Teach students how to find keywords.

- ✦ Give concrete examples.

- ✦ Group items into categories for students to learn.

- ✦ Divide long sections of text into smaller passages.

- ✦ Discuss the questions in the book as a class, and then have students read the text. Review with questions again, if desired.

- ✦ Clarify text (pg. 55).

- ✦ Explain unfamiliar words, multiple-meaning words, signal words, or transition words.

- ✦ Use visual aids, including diagrams (pg. 44).

- ✦ Use manipulatives, gestures, or drawings.

- ✦ Use concept maps to help students describe their ideas about a topic in a pictorial way. Begin with a specific word or problem, and then add descriptive words associated with it. The following is an example:

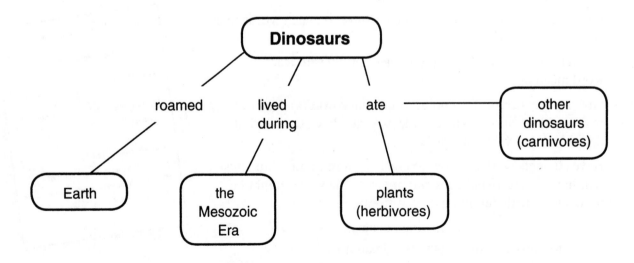

Across the Curriculum (cont.)
Reading Activities

ELLs benefit from reading methods and strategies used with native English speakers. However, they need additional support in vocabulary development, fluency, and motivation. Some aspects of language that native English speakers learn indirectly affect the ease with which ELLs learn to read in English. Consider the factors below when planning lessons, and use the provided tips and activities to increase comprehension.

Factors that affect students learning to read English include the folowing:

- unfamiliar vocabulary
- use of idioms in texts
- figurative language, including imagery and symbolism
- homophones and homographs

- "exceptions to the rules" in grammar
- word order
- sentence structure

General Tips

- Modify instruction using visual, kinesthetic, or concrete references so that students can see or touch.
- Have students read a series of texts with the same characters, plotline, and conflict.
- Use a variety of print materials, such as the following, to give students plenty of practice:
  - instructions
  - handouts
  - newspapers
  - magazines
  - song lyrics
  - letters
  - short stories
  - recipes
- Select reading materials of interest to students, such as these:
  - comic books
  - stories
  - poems
  - nonfiction texts
  - multicultural literature

Teach students how to do the following:

* preview reading material.

* locate topic sentences.

* find supporting details.

* identify introductions and conclusions.

* read nonfiction genres.

* draw conclusions or predict outcomes.

* understand story themes and endings.

* skim to find facts.

Pre-Reading Activities

* Preview and discuss new vocabulary, including words that are not always used in conversation.

* Preview text for words with multiple meanings or idioms.

* Preview sentence structure.

* Build text-specific knowledge by describing characters, ideas, or concepts.

* Use pre-questioning and predictions to set the direction and purpose for reading.

* Draw on students' background knowledge.

* Relate reading to students' lives.

Post-Reading Activities

* Reteach difficult words and concepts.

* Use oral-reading activities to communicate understanding and comprehension of text that students read silently.

* Use a story chart to have students identify the themes in a story. Ask students what the main character was trying to do.

* Read a selection more than once, and discuss a different aspect of the text each time.

* Discuss sequence to understand when and why things happen in a story.

* Have students talk about and summarize the text in small groups or as a class.

Across the Curriculum *(cont.)*
Writing Activities

Writing requires the ability to process language to communicate ideas. Writing helps students remember what they thought about a text; it enables them to respond to what they read.

Students' cultural backgrounds and previous educational experiences may influence how they approach the task of writing. In some cultures, students submit their "rough drafts" as "final copies" for the teacher to correct. These students will not be familiar with our writing process, in which students revise their rough drafts and write final copies before turning in the assignment. In other cultures, students adopt a storytelling style, in which much background information is introduced before getting to the main point. These students will need direct instruction in organizing writing for different purposes.

General Tips

✦ Use writing as a learning tool to promote language development.

✦ Scaffold students (pg. 40) as they learn to write in English.

✦ Match writing activities to ELL development needs.

✦ Provide authentic purposes for writing.

✦ Guide students through the process of writing down what they say. This helps them make connections between oral and written language.

✦ Use props to get students started with the theme or topic for writing.

✦ Use sequenced pictures or other visual aids (pg. 44) for writing.

✦ Introduce games to help students develop word knowledge and spelling skills.

✦ Suggest authentic publishing options for student writing.

✦ Allow students to dictate their ideas first, if necessary.

✦ Allow students to make choices in what they write (e.g., notes to friends or parents, stories).

✦ Have students look at examples that begin with a topic idea and have an ending that lets the reader know the writer is finished.

Across the Curriculum *(cont.)*

Writing Activities *(cont.)*

Pre- and Post-Reading Activities

✦ Introduce a variety of types of writing. Have students experiment with the following:

- • wordless picture books to encourage students to write and develop their own story lines.
- • journal writing for personal expression.
- • poetry writing to learn expressive language.
- • descriptive writing to include a main idea and details.
- • comparative writing to compare and contrast concepts or stories.

✦ Model the writing process and talk with students about what you are writing. Show examples, if desired.

✦ Use brainstorming activities (pg. 27) to generate a list of ideas for writing. Use one or more of these ideas as a starting point for a writing activity.

✦ Have students copy sentences or paragraphs to learn language structure.

✦ Offer cloze activities (pg. 28) for students to express their ideas using learned vocabulary or a word bank.

✦ Conduct a shared writing activity after students have participated in a class experience. Invite students to say sentences about the experience. Then write them exactly as stated on the board. When the story is complete, discuss any changes needed.

✦ Have students write on their own and allow them to refer to a text and retell it in their own words.

✦ Engage students in writing simple sentences about a text they have read or a topic of current class discussion. Continue the activity using these steps:

1. Ask questions to get students started thinking about the topic.
2. Have students express their answers orally.
3. Repeat what students say, modeling correct grammar.
4. Ask students to repeat your corrected sentence.
5. Then have students write the sentence(s) on paper.
6. Have students read aloud exactly what they have written to see if it sounds right.

✦ Have students write in response to a prompt.

✦ Teach students how to participate in free-writing activities:

- • Write for a set amount of time.
- • Do not stop writing.
- • Keep writing, even if you don't know what to write.

Across the Curriculum *(cont.)*
Social Studies Activities

Social studies, by definition, relates to one or more specific cultures. ELLs may not have the cultural background knowledge necessary to understand social studies texts. Some concepts, such as privacy, personal property, and democracy vary from culture to culture, and ELLs may need direct instruction.

General Tips

+ Apply academic standards to textbooks and other social studies reading materials and make connections using keywords and concepts.

+ Break text into smaller parts with visual diagrams.

+ Teach students how to take notes.

+ Have students use visualization techniques (pg. 71) as they read.

+ Help ELLs make connections to their own lives and experiences so they can remember what they've learned.

+ Encourage ELLs to talk with family members in their native languages about what they are learning in social studies.

+ Provide a safe environment in which students can express their opinions.

+ Help students understand and use primary and secondary sources.

Pre-Reading Activities

+ Provide background knowledge about U.S. history, geography, and current events.

+ Introduce students to unfamiliar historical terms and vocabulary.

+ Preteach, demonstrate, and explain idioms and phrases.

+ Refer to "Understanding Nonfiction Text Structures" (pp. 64–68) to preview and introduce text features before students read.

+ Help students understand movement within the structure of a society (e.g., moving from a rural area to an urban area).

+ Provide plenty of practice with map skills, as ELLs may be unfamiliar with maps.

+ Use guided reading strategies (pg. 32) to help ELLs comprehend content.

+ Explain how to tell what is important in a text.

Across the Curriculum *(cont.)*
Social Studies Activities *(cont.)*

Post-Reading Activities

✦ Paraphrase sections of text during class discussions (pg. 62).

✦ Clarify meaning by replacing pronouns with nouns to help students understand what they read.

✦ Provide sentence frames (pg. 40), such as the following, to support students in reading and writing:

- I can change _____ about my community because _____.

- I already know _____ about _____ (topic).

- This _____ (group of people) did _____ because _____.

✦ Invite students to write reflective paragraphs.

✦ Have students answer simple questions.

✦ Have students participate in role-playing exercises.

✦ Use if-then sentences to teach cause and effect.

Across the Curriculum *(cont.)*
Science Activities

Science presents a challenge for many students. This subject introduces complex concepts and vocabulary words not used in everyday conversations. Even though hands-on learning can help ELLs, science experiments may contain detailed steps that are hard for students to understand.

General Tips

✦ Help students understand the "hands-on" approach.

✦ Introduce ELLs to science equipment (e.g., magnifying glasses, balances) and give expectations for classroom behavior.

✦ Introduce students to specific text structures used in science reading material.

✦ Rephrase difficult sentence structure and passive voice, if possible.

✦ Explain visuals in text. Create simplified visuals, if necessary.

✦ Clarify meaning with diagrams.

✦ Cover material more slowly.

✦ Break science passages into "chunks," or smaller sections.

✦ Introduce students to the scientific method.

　　• Help students understand the concept of hypothesis.

　　• Teach students how and why to form conclusions.

✦ Give directions for experiments and procedures in simplified steps.

✦ Help students with vocabulary. Some words have different meanings in science (e.g., *work, power*) than they do in other subjects.

✦ Help students learn the language of science (words and concepts such as *observe, describe, compare, classify, evaluate, conclude, record*, etc.).

✦ Teach students how and why they will work in cooperative groups (pg. 28).

Pre- and Post-Reading Activities

✦ As a class, discuss previous science experiences, including those outside of class (e.g., weather). Have students write and draw about their experiences related to the topic at hand.

✦ Teach the parts of a science experiment, which include the following:

- overview/objectives
- materials
- preparation
- hypothesis
- procedure
- discussion
- record sheet
- conclusion

✦ Provide hands-on activities (pg. 32) to introduce a unit.

✦ Prepare flash cards to help students learn words and the relationship between terms.

✦ Use games to teach new vocabulary words.

✦ Use closed-captioning on science videos to give students visual word clues to accompany new vocabulary they hear.

✦ Use visual aids (pg. 44) to help students understand a process or a conclusion.

✦ Have students explain the processes or concepts to each other. If necessary, students may use their native languages to explain complex concepts to each other first.

✦ Have students use Venn diagrams to compare two methods, processes, or outcomes.

✦ Display results using charts.

✦ Provide sentence frames (pg. 40), such as "If I did this experiment again, I would _____." (In other words, how would you change the experiment?)

✦ Have students work in small groups to discuss ideas, exchange information, and ask questions.

Across the Curriculum *(cont.)*
Sample Lesson: Cross Telling

> ## Objective of the Listening, Speaking, or Reading Lesson
> Students will develop listening skills and increase reading comprehension by orally retelling a reading passage. Use lesson with reading groups, if possible.

Materials

reading passage, one per student

Preparation

1. Select a reading passage, and decide which students will read or retell the various portions of the passage.

2. Create a sentence frame related to the reading selection to use in the opening alphabet memory game activity.

Opening

1. Have students play an alphabet memory game. The first person will say a sentence that includes an item beginning with the letter A. The second person will repeat the sentence, adding an additional item beginning with the letter B, and so on. For example, students could say, "I'm going on a trip and I'm taking a(n) _____." Alternatively, they could say, "I went to the zoo and I saw a(n) _____." Write the sentence frame on the board for students to refer to as they play the game. If possible, use a sentence frame related to the reading passage.

2. Encourage students to notice how they have to listen carefully to what others say in order to stay in the game.

Directions

1. Explain that each student will use listening skills to tell about what someone else has read aloud.

2. Have students take turns reading parts of a passage aloud.

3. After one or two students have read, call on someone to retell what has been read. Retelling what another student has read forces students to listen more carefully and think about what the text actually says.

Closing

1. Have each student state one thing he or she remembers from the overall selection and tell what helped him or her remember that detail.

2. Have students write their sentences and draw sketches to illustrate them.

ELL Tips

✦ Provide keywords to prompt students when they retell.

✦ Point to related pictures to help students remember what other students read.

✦ Create cloze sentences as students express their sentences orally in the closing exercise. Write down the first letter of keywords to help students remember what they said when they write their words on paper.

Across the Curriculum (cont.)
Sample Lesson: Making Inferences

Objective of the Reading Lesson

Students will learn that readers use clues in the text to understand what the author is trying to say.

Materials

- ✦ picture book(s), one per student or one copy for class display
- ✦ content-area textbook (social studies or science), one per student
- ✦ "Context Clue Cards" (pg. 70) (optional)
- ✦ sticky notes (optional)

Opening

Introduce the concept of making inferences with a simple diagram:

> what you read + what you already know
>
> = making inferences

Write it on the board, a piece of chart paper, or an overhead transparency; or display on an interactive whiteboard.

Directions, Part I

Model a think-aloud, demonstrating how to use context clues (pg. 69; cards, pg. 70 [optional]) to infer meaning. For example: "When I read, I can use clues in the text to understand what the author wants to say. So, if the text says that Jessica is excited because her family is going to the mountain cabin, I use my knowledge about what it means to be excited. If I am excited about something, I am looking forward to it because I think I might like it. I can infer that Jessica will have fun at the cabin. The author doesn't tell us what Jessica will do at the cabin, but we know she wants to go there. Often, we like to go places where we know we will have fun."

Directions, Part II

1. Display an illustration from a story, for example, a picture of a man frowning or looking angry. Read aloud a sentence or two that describes something that happened. Ask students how the character feels about the action or event. Explain that students can use pictures to infer what the author means.

2. Have students read a sentence or two from a textbook, for example, a social studies textbook. Have them mark text (pp. 35–36), using sticky notes (if desired) to comment on context clues and inferences.

Directions, Part II *(cont.)*

3. If the text reads, "The leaders needed to get money. They made the people pay taxes," ask students why money is important. Students can infer the meaning of the text by using their knowledge of what a specific word (e.g., *money*) means.

4. Invite students to use their prior knowledge and understanding of the concept (e.g., money) to discuss and add details.

Closing

1. Assign students a passage to read in a story or textbook. Have students write a couple of sentences telling what they know from their reading. Remind students that they can use the following clues to infer meaning:

   - pictures

   - meanings of specific words

   - what is already known about the topic

2. Call on several students to read their sentences to the class. Ask volunteers to give examples of how they used the skill of inference to understand what they stated about the reading passage.

ELL Tip

Allow ELLs to work with one or two other students to read the assigned passage. Have them rehearse one or two statements about the reading before writing their sentences. Have them read their sentences with their partner(s) before calling the class back together.

Across the Curriculum *(cont.)*
Sample Lesson: Finding Information

Objective of the Reading, Science, or Social Studies Lesson

Students will preview words and pictures and then read a sample passage, locating specific information in the passage by matching pictures to facts.

Materials

✦ word cards and related pictures, one set of pictures per student

✦ "Native American Foods" (reading level 3.4) and "Fact-Finding Questions" (pg. 90), one copy per student

✦ glue

✦ sample reading passage from textbook or other curriculum with related word cards, pictures, and questions (optional)

Preparation

1. Prepare word cards by printing one word on each card. Provide a picture (from the Internet, magazines, or other clip-art sources) to accompany each card. Examples of words for the word cards are *salmon, cliff, spear, rabbit, corn, pumpkin,* and *berries.*

2. Photocopy pictures (or print out clip art) providing a set for each student.

3. Use glue to make the pictures into stickers, or have students use glue as they complete the fact-finding task.

4. Optional: Prepare a sample reading passage from a textbook or other classroom resource, related word cards and pictures, and related questions.

Opening

1. Use the word cards and pictures to introduce keywords from the reading passage.

2. Tell students that they will read a sample passage and practice finding information about what they read.

Directions, Part I

1. Discuss with students what happens when they read nonfiction text. They might read more slowly, stop to understand new words, not remember or not understand everything they read, etc.

2. Model a think-aloud (pp. 42–43), explaining that because of the way nonfiction is written, it can be difficult to remember everything that is read.

3. Have students turn and talk with partners to answer the question "How do you find the answer to a question in what you read?"

4. Invite partners to share their ideas with the class. Compile a list of strategies for finding information for student reference.

Across the Curriculum *(cont.)*
Sample Lesson: Finding Information *(cont.)*

Directions, Part II

1. Distribute copies of "Native American Foods" and "Fact-Finding Questions." Have students read the passage in small groups or with partners.

2. Give each student a set of pictures (stickers).

3. Have students place the appropriate picture next to each sentence in the reading passage that answers a specific question. For example, to answer the first question, students should place pictures of corn and pumpkins next to the sentence that states, "They grew corn, beans, and pumpkins."

4. After students have correctly placed the pictures in the reading passage, have them write one-word answers for the questions.

Closing

1. Challenge students to rewrite their answers to the questions using complete sentences.

2. Optional: Have students repeat the exercise with one or more paragraphs from a textbook or other classroom resource. If applicable, have students also write the page number where they located the facts or information.

ELL Tips

✦ Provide sentence frames during the closing activity, if needed.

✦ Work with a small group of students to help them place the pictures correctly within the reading passage.

Native American Foods

Native Americans ate many types of foods. Some people lived by rivers or the ocean. They caught salmon or other fish with spears or nets. Those by the ocean used harpoons to catch whales. Some tribes hunted game. They hunted bison and deer. Natives worked together to drive large animals into a pit or over a cliff. Sometimes, they set fires or built fences. Then the animals could not escape. Other tribes set traps for rabbits or other game. People used bows and arrows, spears, and other tools to hunt.

Some native tribes grew crops. They grew corn, beans, and pumpkins. They grew potatoes and sunflowers. They gathered berries, roots, nuts, and seeds. Some people dried berries and other foods to keep through the winter. Native people ate the foods that they could find and did not waste anything. They used resources well.

Fact-Finding Questions

1. What did Native Americans catch in the water?

2. How did natives hunt game?

3. What is one animal the natives ate for meat?

4. Name two crops some native tribes grew.

5. What food could people gather that grew wild?

Across the Curriculum (cont.)
Sample Lesson: It's My Story

Objective of the Writing Lesson

Students will discuss family stories at home and with classmates to understand the differences and similarities between stories.

Materials

✦ sample picture-book story

✦ sample nonfiction text

Preparation

Have students think about and discuss with family members stories that have been handed down in their families. Students should take notes or draw pictures to help them remember the stories. Encourage students to bring their stories (and notes) to class to share.

Opening

1. Ask students to think about what they know about writing. Provide sentence frames, such as the following, if necessary:

   • I know that writing is _____.

   • People write to _____.

2. Have students discuss their responses in small groups.

3. Conduct a class discussion about what students know about writing and stories.

Directions, Part I

1. Have volunteers take turns telling stories that have been told to multiple generations in their families.

2. Write down some student stories, and explore the differences in the ways people tell stories.

3. Remind students that we would not want to read stories that are all the same. We like to read different kinds of stories written by different authors.

4. Compare and contrast these differences with a sample American picture book story that has a topic sentence, clear plot, and a main idea or central message.

5. Create a "What We Notice" chart to outline basic conventions used in English writing, such as the following:

   • title

   • topic sentence

   • plot

   • characters

   • dialogue

   • a problem that the main character solves

Across the Curriculum *(cont.)*
Sample Lesson: It's My Story *(cont.)*

Directions, Part II

1. Discuss as a whole group the concept of having a clear message in writing. Use the picture-book story or page of nonfiction text as an example. Ask the following questions:

   - What does the author want to say?

   - How do you know?

2. Have students think again about their family stories. Ask them to turn and talk with partners about why they want to tell those stories. Have them use the following sentence frames:

   - I want to tell this story because _____.

   - I want to say _____ about _____.

   - This is important to me because _____.

Closing

1. Guide students through the process of writing down what they say. As time allows, select one or more student stories to use as examples or use your own family story to model. Say a sentence aloud to begin telling the story, and then write it on the board.

2. Have students work with partners to dictate or help each other write their simple stories on paper. Remind them that their classmates will be their audience.

3. Encourage students to edit each others' work as time allows.

4. Have students use any drawings they made in preparation for the lesson as illustrations for their stories.

ELL Tips

✦ Remind all students to speak slowly and clearly when sharing their stories with the class.

✦ Use specific gestures to indicate items to include in the "What We Notice" chart.

✦ Use the sentence frames provided.

Across the Curriculum *(cont.)*
Sample Lesson: Thinking Like a Scientist

Objective of the Science Lesson

Students will observe a demonstration, make predictions, test their hypotheses in a whole-group or small-group setting, and write simple conclusions.

Materials

- ✦ several pieces of scrap paper
- ✦ word cards: *observe, hypothesis, conclusion;* optional word card for *gravity*

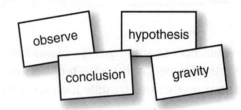

Opening

1. Conduct a demonstration by dropping a piece of paper from desk height. Ask students what they saw. (Sample answer: A piece of paper fell to the floor.)

2. Display the word card for *observe.* Drop another piece of paper, and ask students to watch carefully to see what happens.

3. Introduce the word by asking the class what they observed.

4. Ask a volunteer to define the word based on how you just used it in a sentence related to an action. (Sample answer: To observe something means to watch it very carefully.)

Directions, Part I

1. Tell students that today they will learn to think like scientists. They will learn some scientific words, such as the word they just learned in the opening activity.

2. Display the word card for *hypothesis.* Have students talk with partners about what they think the word means.

3. Invite students to share their thoughts with the class. Take notes on the board to record words or phrases students suggest.

4. Ask a volunteer to come up and fold a piece of paper three times (into eighths).

5. Have another volunteer hold a piece of unfolded paper.

6. Ask the class which piece of paper they think will reach the floor first when dropped from the same height.

7. Ask what word students already know that means "to say what you think will happen" (Sample answers: *predict, to make a prediction*). Make a connection between the word *predict* and any related words students suggested earlier when they brainstormed the word *hypothesis.* Explain that this science word means "to make a prediction."

8. Have the class observe what they notice about how the two pieces of paper are different. (Sample answers: One is folded, one is not; the folded piece of paper is now a smaller size; the person holding it may observe that the folded piece of paper feels heavier.)

Directions, Part I *(cont.)*

9. Write one or more sentence frames, such as the following, on the board (depending on the level of challenge desired) to help students form a hypothesis.

   • I think the _____ (folded, unfolded) piece of paper will fall to the floor first.

   • The _____ (folded, unfolded) piece of paper will fall to the floor first because _____.

10. Have volunteers or small groups of students conduct the experiment. Repeat with different sizes or weights of paper or different numbers of folds in the paper, if desired. Encourage students to adjust their predictions (restate their hypotheses) accordingly.

Directions, Part II

1. Ask the class if anyone knows the science word to describe the answer to the hypothesis, or how the prediction turned out.

2. Display the *conclusion* card and discuss how a conclusion tells what happened. (Sample answers: Conclusions should answer the question and say how the experiment shows the hypothesis is true or false.)

3. Have students work with partners to write simple sentences that answer the question(s) posed by the class about one of the falling paper experiments. Instruct students to use the following sentence frames:

   • The _____ (folded, unfolded) piece of paper fell to the floor first because _____.

   • When we used a _____ (folded, unfolded) piece of paper, _____ happened.

   • Next time, I will try _____.

Closing

1. Invite students to write simple definitions and illustrate the new science words they learned.

2. Create a class display for future reference.

ELL Tips

✦ Work with ELLs in small groups to go over definitions of the new vocabulary words.

✦ Review the concept of gravity, if necessary.

✦ Review the new vocabulary words in subsequent lessons.

Across the Curriculum *(cont.)*
Sample Lesson: Taking Notes

Objective of the Reading, Science, or Social Studies Lesson
Students will review a reading selection to practice recalling information and taking notes about what they read.

Materials

- sample picture or photograph, large enough for class display
- several sample reading passages, such as those found in leveled readers, science or social studies texts, short stories, etc.
- crayons or colored pencils (optional)
- "Content Clue Cards" (pg. 70)

Opening

1. Draw a web on the board. In the center circle, write the title of a story or nonfiction passage all the students have recently read.

2. Have students contribute words or phrases to describe the main idea of the reading passage.

3. Review how a graphic organizer such as this can help us remember what we read.

Directions, Part I

1. Explain that a "note" is a word or phrase you write down to remind you of something you read. It can also be a picture you draw to remind you what the reading is about. (*Note:* Some students may say a note is a short letter. Explain that in this lesson you are using the word in a different way.)

2. Display a picture or photograph. Have students write simple words or phrases to describe what they see. Ask volunteers to share their responses with the class. Tell students that this is one simple way to take notes to remember something.

3. Model how to take notes as you read a brief science or social studies passage. After reading a paragraph, stop and think aloud. Example: "This paragraph tells me what animals need to live. I can write the words *air, water,* and *shelter.* The next paragraph talks about how different animals run, fly, or jump to hunt. I can draw a picture of one or more of the animals. I can write the word *hunt* next to the picture. Next, I read about what these animals eat. I can draw pictures of what they eat and write the word *food* next to the picture. My words and drawings will help me remember what I read even after I put the book away."

Directions, Part II

1. Give students different sample reading passages. Have them read the passages once. Then have them read them again and write down keywords or phrases or draw pictures to describe or show the main ideas of the passages.

2. Collect the papers.

Across the Curriculum *(cont.)*

Sample Lesson: Taking Notes *(cont.)*

Directions, Part II *(cont.)*

3. Select a sample student paper and read the notes aloud to the class or show the picture(s). Tell what you think that person read. Example: "This paper has a drawing of a butterfly with arrows and some other drawings. I wonder if the person read about the life cycle of a butterfly."

4. Redistribute student papers (anonymously, if possible) to the class.

5. Have students work in groups of two or three to read their classmates' notes and discuss what that person might have read.

Closing

Review what students have learned about using context clues (pg. 69) to understand what they read. Have students use "Context Clue Cards" and identify which clue(s) they used most when reading to take notes and remember what they read.

ELL Tips

✦ During the opening activity, review the illustrations from the sample reading selection to help ELLs remember the story.

✦ When students write words to describe the pictures they observe, allow them to dictate their words or write in their native languages.

✦ Have students work with partners to complete the reading and note-taking assignment.

Across the Curriculum *(cont.)*
Sample Lesson: Community Helpers

Objective of the Social Studies Lesson

Students will learn new vocabulary, understand the role of community helpers, and write letters to individuals who work in the community.

Materials

- ✦ pictures of community services in your area, for example, a local fire station, police station, library, bus station, hospital, etc.
- ✦ textbook pages or other reading selections related to community helpers

Opening

1. Display pictures of community helpers and services one at a time. Invite students to identify each using English or their native languages.

2. Ask students to state what the people who work for each place do (e.g., Doctors help people feel better using medicine.). Have ELLs use individual whiteboards or come up to the board to draw pictures showing people working at jobs. Discuss as a class.

Directions, Part I

Have students work in groups of three, with low-level ELLs grouped with students who have greater proficiency in English. Encourage students to help each other discuss their responses to the following questions:

- ✦ How do these people help our community?
- ✦ Why are they important?
- ✦ How are these types of people important in my culture?
- ✦ How can I tell them they are important to our community?

Directions, Part II

1. Read the textbook pages aloud. Stop after each community helper word (e.g., *firefighter, police officer, librarian, postal worker*), and have students repeat the word(s).

2. As a class, have students share the ideas they discussed in their small groups. Encourage ELLs to participate as well, since they have practiced, or rehearsed, their thoughts in a small group and have received assistance.

3. Ask ELLs to share the role these and other types of community helpers play in their own cultures.

Directions, Part III

1. Assist students as they write a simple letter to a community helper.

2. Have students thank the person for one thing he or she does to help the community.

Across the Curriculum *(cont.)*

Sample Lesson: Community Helpers *(cont.)*

Directions, Part III *(cont.)*

3. If desired, provide a model on the board for ELLs to follow. Encourage them to recall the ideas they discussed in their small groups. Repeat specific phrases as necessary to help students write simple sentences.

Closing

Invite students to role-play how community helpers help in the local community. Encourage students to share something new they learned about community helpers after talking with their classmates.

ELL Tips

✦ Use pictures to aid the discussion and help students learn new vocabulary words.

✦ When reading the textbook pages or other reading passages, use choral reading techniques (pg. 27).

✦ Have students use their native languages to initially discuss community helpers.

✦ Allow students to verbalize ideas before writing their letters.

Across the Curriculum *(cont.)*
Sample Lesson: Taking a Test

Objective of the Lesson
Students will read a short passage and practice taking notes to answer sample test questions.

Materials

✦ "Cantor's Giant Soft-Shelled Turtles" (reading level 2.6; 118 words) (pg. 101) or similar passage, one copy per student and one copy for class display

✦ scrap paper, one piece per student

✦ sample test (pg. 102), one copy per student and one copy for class display

Opening

1. Display the sample test. Ask the following questions to engage students in a discussion about taking a test.

   • How does this test look the same as other tests you have seen? How does it look different?
   • What makes a test easy?
   • What is the hardest thing about taking a test?
   • What can you tell others to help them take a test?

2. Take note of differences in ELLs' background knowledge and expectations regarding tests.

Directions, Part I

1. Display the reading passage and distribute copies to the class. Read through the passage together, using a strategy from "Reading Activities" (pp. 77–78).

2. Give each student a piece of scrap paper. Tell students that they will use the scrap paper to take notes instead of marking on the reading passage. Explain that often they will not be able to write on a test.

3. Ask students to identify keywords, the main idea, and details. Have students write related keywords and phrases on their pieces of scrap paper.

4. Tell the class that another way to remember what they read is to take notes on graphic organizers. Draw a simple web on the board.

5. Have a volunteer write the main idea (soft-shelled turtles) in the center circle. Ask students to complete other circles on the web with details related to the main idea. Ask students how this information might help them answer questions. (Sample answer: They can look for those keywords in the answer choices to help them find the correct answers.)

6. Have students read the passage again silently or with partners.

Directions, Part II

1. Distribute copies of the sample test.

2. Preview the test, reviewing how to read directions and mark answer choices clearly. Remind students to read questions carefully, read all the answer choices, and find the best answer (by eliminating the wrong answers, if necessary).

Directions, Part II *(cont.)*

3. Go through the test together, discussing how to answer each question. Use this as an activity to have students learn about taking tests, not just finding the correct answers for this particular test.

   - *Question #1* is a compare/contrast question. Students can use what they already know about turtles (background knowledge) to find the best answer. Many students will picture turtles as having a hard shell; the soft shell is a clear difference.

   - *Question #2* asks students to recall a particular detail. Only one color word listed here is mentioned in the reading. If a detail question contained more than one word mentioned in a reading passage, students could read the detail in context to determine if it answers the question.

   - *Question #3* asks students to use context clues to answer the vocabulary question. They will have to read the details in the sentence to understand the context, a turtle's body. They can also substitute the answer choices in the sentence to determine which one makes the most sense.

   - *Question #4* asks students to identify the main idea of the reading passage. If necessary, guide students through marking text (pp. 35–36) or taking notes to locate keywords or phrases that show the overall main idea of the passage.

   - *Question #5* asks students to make inferences. Point out sentences in the last paragraph that indicate that there are not as many soft-shelled turtles now as there used to be. Refer to earlier questions and review the fact that these turtles are set apart because they have soft shells, thus eliminating answer choices B and D. Read the sentences about their claws, jaws, and quick bites to eliminate the statement that the turtles have no enemies.

4. Allow students to complete the sample test individually, filling in the appropriate circles to indicate their answer choices. This gives students practice in reading the questions and answer choices for themselves and marking an answer.

5. If time allows, go over student papers again at a later time, correcting and discussing as needed.

Closing

1. Have students talk with partners about one thing they learned about taking a test in this lesson. Have partners help each other write their ideas on paper.

2. Compile student responses to create a "Test-Taking Tips" class book to encourage students and give them confidence in test-taking situations throughout the year.

ELL Tips

- Break test directions into smaller "chunks."

- Give students another opportunity to practice test-taking skills using a different reading passage.

- Encourage students to use context clues (pg. 69) to answer vocabulary questions.

Cantor's Giant Soft-Shelled Turtles

These soft-shelled turtles live by freshwater streams. They like swamps and mudflats.

Some people call them "frog head" turtles. They are olive-green or brown. They have broad heads. Their eyes are close to the tip of the snout. They have rubbery skin. Ribs fused together protect the inside organs. They grow up to six feet long.

These turtles eat shellfish and other types of fish. Sometimes they eat plants that grow in the water. They burrow in the sand. The turtles come up two times a day to breathe air. They have long claws and strong jaws. The turtles bite quickly.

Soft-shelled turtles are endangered. People hunt them for food and medicine. They live mainly in Cambodia.

Name: _____   Date: _____

Cantor's Giant Soft-Shelled Turtles

Directions: Read the story. Use the story to answer the questions. Fill in the circle next to the correct answer.

1. How are these turtles different from other turtles?
   - Ⓐ They breathe air.
   - Ⓑ They like water.
   - Ⓒ They have soft shells.
   - Ⓓ They have four legs.

2. What color are the turtles?
   - Ⓐ olive-green or brown
   - Ⓑ yellow or blue
   - Ⓒ black or purple
   - Ⓓ red or orange

3. In this passage, the word **organs** means
   - Ⓐ musical instruments.
   - Ⓑ body parts that do a certain job.
   - Ⓒ air bubbles.
   - Ⓓ types of food.

4. This passage is mainly about
   - Ⓐ freshwater streams.
   - Ⓑ what turtles eat.
   - Ⓒ frog heads.
   - Ⓓ soft-shelled turtles.

5. Which sentence is most true?
   - Ⓐ There are not very many soft-shelled turtles.
   - Ⓑ These turtles have a hard shell.
   - Ⓒ These turtles have no enemies.
   - Ⓓ These turtles look just like other turtles.

Cantor's Giant Soft-Shelled Turtles: Test Answers

1. C; They have soft shells.

2. A; olive-green or brown

3. B; body parts that do a certain job

4. D; soft-shelled turtles

5. A; There are not very many soft-shelled turtles.

Across the Curriculum *(cont.)*

Assessment

Assessing what students can and cannot do will help you to create focused learning experiences that are designed to take students to the next step in their learning. Once you have identified your students' needs, present curriculum accordingly. Plan assessments in such a way to allow students to express what they have learned. Assessments should reflect individual student growth, as well as the level at which students have grasped a particular concept or skill.

When planning assessments, be aware your students' . . .

◆ language proficiency levels.

◆ cultural backgrounds.

◆ educational backgrounds.

◆ learning styles.

◆ individual goals and needs.

◆ progress and growth over time.

Use a variety of procedures and techniques to assess students, such as the following:

✦ **Pre-Assessments**

- Oral diagnostics

- Written diagnostics

- Get-to-know-you activities

✦ **Post-Assessments**

- Quick oral check-ups

- Written work over time

- Observation charts or logs

- Student rubrics: Use rubrics to guide students so they can evaluate their own work or behavior.

- Exit tickets: Give students exit tickets. Have them respond orally or in writing to questions or prompts. Students give their tickets to the teacher on their way to another room or activity. Provide feedback as time allows.

- Comfort scale: Ask students to write or show a number of fingers to indicate the level of their understanding. (5 = I understand, 3 = I'm a little confused, 1 = I don't get it)

- Give One, Get One: Have students write or orally rehearse one new fact or piece of information they've learned. Go around the room asking students to add to a list compiled on the board.

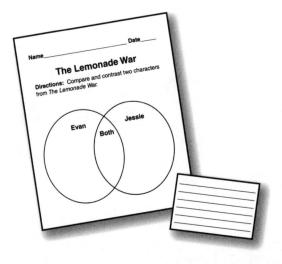

✦ **Pre- and Post-Assessments**

- Graphic organizers (pg. 31)

- Flash cards

- Quick writes or free-writing

- Journals

- Whole-group response (pg. 44)

- Class discussions

Modify assessments as needed.

✦ Focus on student strengths rather than weaknesses.

✦ Measure ELLs' progress individually, rather than measuring against native English speakers, when possible.

✦ Use assessments that don't always rely on student mastery of reading and writing.

✦ Modify test language and jargon.

✦ Simplify sentence structures.

✦ Adapt tests as needed to assess what students should be able to do.

About Follow-up Assessments

Evaluate preliminary assessment results to determine what instruction is now needed to ensure that students meet stated standards or objectives. Write objectives for subsequent lessons that clearly state specific skills and content students should learn. Conduct follow-up assessments based on the following objectives:

✦ Give students appropriate tasks for their learning needs.

✦ Track student progress with ongoing assessments.

✦ Incorporate material already taught at students' levels to measure progress.

✦ Tell students your expectations prior to the lesson.

✦ Model tasks or activities first.

✦ Review assignments with students and check their answers.

Help students to reduce their test anxiety.

✦ Provide encouragement and support for students so they don't experience a fear of failure.

✦ Before testing students, teach them the following:

- the basics—where to write their names, how to follow directions (and read them carefully!), and how to fill in circles correctly

- academic language on standardized tests (e.g., *summarize, name two ways*)

- ways to answer types of test questions

- the difference between facts and opinions

- how to find the main idea

- how to find specific details

- how to make inferences

- how to find keywords and vocabulary

- how to sequence events

- how to compare and contrast

- to read all the answer choices

- how to eliminate wrong answer choices and find the best answer

---

About Standardized Testing

Educators recognize the need for accommodations in standardized testing procedures for students with limited English proficiency. Not all tests allow the same modifications. The questions below will help you determine how accurately a standardized test might measure ELLs' academic progress.

✦ Can teachers allow extra time for ELL students?

✦ Can students use bilingual dictionaries?

✦ Can students take the test in a small-group environment?

✦ Can the test administrator read items orally to students?

✦ Can students respond to questions in their native languages?

✦ Can students use gestures, such as pointing or other physical demonstrations, to show learning?

Across the Curriculum *(cont.)*
Assessment *(cont.)*

Encourage students to monitor their own learning.

✦ Have students complete the following sentence frames:

- I enjoyed learning about _____ because _____.
- Today I learned _____.
- I still need help on _____ because _____.
- I enjoyed talking about _____.
- _____ is another way to solve this problem.
- The hardest thing today was _____.
- I was feeling happy when _____.
- I want to learn more about _____.
- The best part about my project was _____.
- For my next project, I need to remember to _____.
- One of the hardest things about my project was _____.

About Grading

Grades are more than numbers or letters. Grading . . .

✦ is a communication tool that reflects your beliefs about learning.

✦ helps you to design appropriate tasks to meet student-learning needs.

✦ gives students feedback and can request that students respond to feedback.

✦ gives teachers information for teacher/student conferences about specific student work.

✦ can incorporate checklists of increasing competencies.

✦ lets parents know their children's progress.

Teacher Resources
Websites for Educators

Center for Applied Linguistics (CAL): *http://www.cal.org*
CAL publishes research, teacher education, instructional materials, etc., about language, literacy, assessment, and culture. For a complete list of their ELL resources, go to "TOPICS" at the top, left-hand side of the page and select "English Language Learners."

Classroom Zoom: *http://www.classroomzoom.com*
Classroom Zoom is an online subscription service created by Teacher Created Resources. Subscribers to the service have access to more than 11,000 printable lessons—all searchable by grade and subject. Members can also create custom crosswords, word searches, and math worksheets. Additionally, there are more than 1,000 free lessons available to nonmembers.

¡Colorín Colorado!: *http://www.colorincolorado.org*
This is a bilingual site created by WETA (Washington Educational Telecommunications Association) for families and educators of English language learners. It includes useful information, strategies, activities, and resources. Many activities have been designed for children in Pre-K–3 but can be adapted for older grades. Click on the "For Educators" link on the left-hand side to begin exploring many ELL resources.

Dave's ESL Café: *http://www.eslcafe.com*
This site is maintained by its founder, Dave Sperling—a teacher with both ESL and EFL instructional experience. Since 1995, Dave has devoted much time and energy to creating a site dedicated to providing ideas for ESL teachers, as well as support for ELLs. On this site, you can find teacher forums, lesson ideas, sample quizzes, and even job boards.

Everything ESL.net: *http://www.everythingesl.net*
Judie Haynes, an ESL teacher from New Jersey with more than 32 years of experience, is the main contributor to this site, which includes lesson plans, teaching tips, and various resources for ESL teachers. There is also a question-and-answer section where visitors are encouraged to ask questions (to Judie) and give responses.

LEARN NC: *http://www.learnnc.org*
LEARN NC is a program of the University of North Carolina at Chapel Hill School of Education. The site provides lesson plans, professional development opportunities, and innovative web resources to support teachers, build community, and improve K–12 education. To browse articles, tutorials, and books, click on "Best Practices" on the left-hand side.

National Center for Family Literacy (NCFL): *http://www.famlit.org*
NCFL has been promoting family literacy since 1989. It has helped more than one million families by pioneering family literacy programs. For free family and educator resources, including activities, tips, and podcasts, go to "NCFL IN ACTION" on the left-hand side, click on "FREE RESOURCES," and then select the topic of interest at the top of the page. Grant and professional development opportunities can also be found under "NCFL IN ACTION."

National Clearinghouse for English Language Acquisition and Language Instruction Educational Programs (NCELA): *http://www.ncela.gwu.edu*
This site contains information and resources dedicated to Title III (organized by state), standards and assessments, and grants and funding. It also offers webinars, publications (including NCLEA's *AccELLerate*), and a resource library to aid ESL teachers in the classroom. Use the search bar in the upper, right-hand corner of the main page to search by topic and access articles.

Reading Is Fundamental (RIF): *http://www.rif.org*
RIF is the United States's oldest and largest nonprofit children's literacy organization. Since its first distribution in 1966, RIF has continued to give new, free books to at-risk children. (In 2010, RIF gave more than 4 million children 16 million books!) For booklists, articles, and activities that inspire literacy, select "LITERACY RESOURCES" at the top of the page. RIF also provides training and resources to help parents and educators inspire children to read. RIF has 19,000 locations across the U.S. To find a RIF program near you, go to *http://map.rif.org/maps/* and type your ZIP code in the box.

Reading Rockets: *http://www.readingrockets.org*
Reading Rockets, a project created by WETA, is aimed to inform educators and parents on how to teach children to read, why some children struggle with reading, and how adults can help struggling children. The project includes PBS television programs; online resources, such as podcasts and blogs; and professional development opportunities. Strategies, reading guides, and newsletters can also be found on the site. For articles specific to ELLs, go to "Reading Topics A–Z" in the left-hand column and select "English Language Learners."

School Collection, The: Children's Literature at the Education & Social Science Library: *http://www.library.illinois.edu/edx/wordless.htm*
This site, which is maintained by the Education and Social Science Library at the University of Illinois at Urbana-Champaign, lists recommended wordless picture books appropriate for classroom use. The books are sorted by category, such as fantasy and adventure or animals.

Teachers First: *http://www.teachersfirst.com*
Helping educators since 1998, Teachers First offers teachers more than 12,000 classroom and professional resources, including rubrics, lesson plans, and tips for working with parents, substitutes, and technology.

Teaching Diverse Learners (TDL): *http://www.alliance.brown.edu/tdl/index.shtml*
TDL, supported by the Education Alliance at Brown University, is a website dedicated to providing support and resources for ESL teachers. It includes strategies, educational materials, and publications, as well as information on assessment and policy.

United Nations Cyberschoolbus: *http://www.cyberschoolbus.un.org*
This multilingual site offers accurate, official, and up-to-date information and statistics regarding the countries and cultures of the world. Visitors can learn about the history and work of the United Nations, as well as browse through UN publications, listen to webcasts, and read about the latest UN news.

Teacher Resources *(cont.)*
Translation Websites

Bing Translator: *http://www.microsofttranslator.com*
This free translator can translate over 30 languages. Users have the options of copying and pasting text into a box or entering website addresses (for full website translations). Additionally, the site offers Tbot—an automated "buddy" that provides translations for Windows Live Messenger. Using the Tbot translator, friends who speak other languages can have one-on-one conversations. Users simply need to add *mtbot@hotmail.com* to their Messenger contacts.

Dictionary.com Translator: *http://translate.reference.com*
This free translator can translate over 50 languages and up to 140 characters at a time. The site also offers a separate Spanish dictionary and translator. At the top of the page, select "Spanish" to view the translator box, as well as the Spanish word of the day, phrase of the day, and grammar tip of the day. The site contains over 750,000 English-Spanish dictionary definitions, example sentences, synonyms, and audio pronunciations.

Google Translate: *http://translate.google.com*
This free translator can translate over 60 languages. Users have the options of copying and pasting text into a box, uploading entire documents, or entering website addresses (for full website translations).

SDL FreeTranslation.com: *http://www.freetranslation.com*
This free translator can translate over 30 languages. Users have the options of copying and pasting text into a box or entering website addresses (for full website translations). The site also offers audio or emailed translations. A free iPhone application and Facebook translator can also be downloaded.

World Lingo: *http://www.worldlingo.com/en/products_services/worldlingo_translator.html*
This free translator can translate over 30 languages. Users have the options of copying and pasting text into a box, uploading documents, entering website addresses (for website translations), or entering email text (for email translations). Free translations are limited to 500 words.

Yahoo! Babel Fish: *http://babelfish.yahoo.com*
This free translator has a limited language selection; however, the site is very user-friendly. Users have the options of copying and pasting up to 150 words into a box or entering website addresses (for full website translations).

Teacher Resources *(cont.)*
Listening Websites

English Listening Quizzes: *http://esl.about.com/library/quiz/bllisteningquiz.htm*
This website includes more than 40 audio files along with matching quizzes. Quizzes cover a variety of topics, including ordering food, going on a trip, and finding out how much something costs. The language level is provided under each quiz and ranges from beginning to advanced.

Randall's ESL Cyber Listening Lab: *http://www.esl-lab.com*
Randall Davis, an educator with extensive ESL and EFL teaching experience, has been maintaining this website since 1998. The site includes more than 100 audio files (in both children's and adults' voices), as well as matching quizzes. The quizzes are categorized by topic (e.g., general, academic) and level (e.g., easy, medium, difficult) and can be graded electronically. Most quizzes are also accompanied by related pre-listening and post-listening exercises.

Tips for Online Searches

✦ Add "ELL" to any search term to narrow the focus.

✦ Search for any strategy, for example "ELL visualization" or "ELL environmental print."

✦ Look up the following keywords and phrases:

- literacy strategies
- learning styles
- cultural awareness
- culture and customs lessons
- signal words
- common idioms
- wordless picture books
- readers' theater scripts
- graphic organizers
- assessment

Note: Consider locating specific articles and then cutting and pasting the information into text or HTML documents (on a blog) for student use, as some advertisements may be inappropriate for younger students.

Bibliography

Adler, Mortimer J., Ph.D. "How to Mark a Book." The Radical Academy. Accessed July 25, 2011. http://www.tnellen.com/cybereng/adler.html.

Ben-Yosef, Elite. "Respecting Students' Cultural Literacies." *Educational Leadership* 61, no. 2 (October 2003): 80–82.

Fay, Kathleen and Suzanne Whaley. "The Gift of Attention." *Educational Leadership* 62, no. 4 (December 2004/January 2005): 76–79.

Haynes, Judie. "Teach to Students' Learning Styles." Everything ESL.net. Accessed July 25, 2011. http://www.everythingesl.net/inservices/learningstyle.php.

Lessow-Hurley, Judith. "What Educators Need to Know About Language." In *Meeting the Needs of Second Language Learners: An Educator's Guide*. Alexandria, VA: Association for Supervision and Curriculum, 2003.

Nieto, Sonia M. "Profoundly Multicultural Questions." *Educational Leadership* 60, no. 4 (December 2002/January 2003): 6–10.

Opitz, Michael F., and Lindsey M. Guccione. *Comprehension and English Language Learners*. Portsmouth, NH: Heinemann, 2009.

Project G.L.A.D. Accessed July 25, 2011. http://www.projectglad.com/

Quindlen, Terrey Hatcher. "Reaching Minority Students: Strategies for Closing the Achievement Gap." *Education Update* 44, no. 5 (August 2002).

Ren Dong, Yu. "Getting at the Content." *Educational Leadership* 62, no. 4 (December 2004/January 2005): 14–19.

Reyes, Carmen Y. "When Students Don't Get It: Helping Low Achieving Students Understand Concepts." Teacher Planet. December 29, 2009. Accessed July 25, 2011. http://www.news4teachers.com/When_Students_%20Dont_Get_It.php.

Sapon-Shevin, Mara. "Schools Fit for All." *Educational Leadership* 58, no. 4 (December 2000/January 2001): 34–39.

Simkins, Michael, Karen Cole, Fern Tavalin, and Barbara Means. "Making a Real World Connection." Chapter 3 in *Increasing Student Learning through Multimedia Projects*. Alexandria, VA: Association for Supervision and Curriculum Development, 2002.

Stephens, Peter. "How to Mark a Book." *Slow Reads Blog*. http://slowreads.com/ResourcesHowToMarkABook-Outline.htm.

TESOL. *TESOL ESL Standards for Pre-K–12 Students*. Alexandria, VA: TESOL, 1997.

Tomlinson, Carol Ann. "Grading for Success." *Educational Leadership* 58, no. 6 (March 2001): 12–15.

WIDA. "WIDA Performance Definitions." WIDA Consortium. Accessed July 25, 2011. http://www.wida.us/standards/PerfDefs.pdf.